CENTENER

Published by
Princeton Architectural Press
A division of Chronicle Books LLC
70 West 36th Street
New York, NY 10018
papress.com

Printed and bound in India
26 25 24 23   4 3 2 1 First edition

Editor: Sara Stemen
Designers: Paul Wagner and
Natalie Snodgrass
Front cover design: Adolphus
Washington and Kaleena Sales

Typeset in Dapifer by Joshua Darden,
Martin by Tré Seals, and Cabinet
Grotesk by Indian Type Foundry.
Chapter numerals and drop caps derived
from a typeface by Adolphus
Washington.

Library of Congress
Cataloging-in-Publication Data
Names: Sales, Kaleena, editor.
Title: Centered : people and ideas
  diversifying design / edited by
  Kaleena Sales.
Other titles: Centered (Princeton
  Architectural Press) Description: First
  edition. | New York : Princeton
  Architectural Press, [2023] | Includes
  bibliographical references. |
Summary: "A collection of beautifully
  illustrated essays and interviews
  presenting a rich, inclusive,
  contemporary, and global vision of
  design diversity"—Provided by
  publisher
Identifiers: LCCN 2022057546 |
  ISBN 9781797223629 (paperback) |
  ISBN 9781797226934 (ebook)
Subjects: LCSH: Design—Social aspects.
Classification: LCC NK1520 .C39 2023 |
  DDC 744—dc23/eng/20221221
  LC record available at https://lccn.
  loc.gov/2022057546

CENTERED

People + Ideas
Diversifying Design

Edited by **Kaleena Sales**

PA PRESS

PRINCETON ARCHITECTURAL PRESS · NEW YORK

CONTENTS

INTRODUCTION

Kaleena Sales

My interest in design history is largely rooted in a concern for social justice and equity. As a design professor and department chair at an HBCU (Historically Black College and University), I work mostly with Black students who are seeking a career in art and design. My students—and all students, regardless of background or identity—deserve to be taught about design from an inclusive, diverse, and global perspective. For too long, the industry has not concerned itself with inclusion. Our curriculum, industry awards, and portfolio criteria are overwhelmingly Eurocentric, perpetuating systemic exclusion for anyone not able or willing to comply with its conventions.

Although cultures from around the world have been creating visual communication and solving complex design problems since the start of humanity, the early twentieth-century modernist movement ushered in a style that has furnished the fundamental guiding principles for contemporary graphic design. The style was exemplified by the teachers and students of the Staatliches Bauhaus, the German art school founded in Weimar in 1919 by the architect Walter Gropius. The use of clean lines, grids, asymmetrical compositions, and sans serif typefaces reflected European philosophies surrounding technology, industrialization, and the arts. Notably, modernism deemed decorative elements and adornments as insubstantial—a belief at odds with many cultures around the world, whose ornamental designs hold symbolic meaning.

The development of the Gutenberg press and later manufacturing advances during the Industrial Revolution contributed to Europe's success in establishing itself as a beacon of innovation. However, the story of European cultural dominance would not be complete without sharing the realities and impact that colonialism, slavery, and genocide have had on cultures and communities across the globe. When we teach from a singular narrative, we are complicit in perpetuating a whitewashed version of design history that uncritically glorifies European accomplishments.

As the design industry works to decenter Eurocentric ideologies and wrestles with its conventional practices, this book advocates including new and diverse work in the canon. The essays and interviews center people, places, methods, ideas, and beliefs that have been eclipsed by dominant design movements. In doing so, this book also centers the lived experiences of those cultures and communities whose voices have been quieted because of colonial dominance. The intention is not to discredit or denounce the work of Swiss design, the Bauhaus, or any other modernist movements but to pursue balance in the way that we remember and honor global contributions to design. This book is for practitioners, educators, students, and anyone interested in expanding narratives and gaining a more inclusive understanding of design.

This book has its origins in *Beyond the Bauhaus*, a series of short essays I developed through my board service with AIGA's Design Educators Community

Steering Committee in 2019. My goal with that series was to amplify design work from underrepresented groups who have been left out of the design canon. The first article featured the beautifully designed West African Adinkra symbols from the Akan people of Côte d'Ivoire and discussed the deep meaning within the symbols, as well as the use of common visual principles within the designs. What I hoped to demonstrate to readers was that there were examples of sophisticated, intelligent design in many cultures around the world, many of which were developed prior to movements like the Bauhaus. The next essay was on the work of AfriCOBRA, a Civil Rights–era artist collective based in Chicago. While the work of AfriCOBRA has made its impact within the fine arts scene, gaining notoriety during the height of the Black Power Movement, I sought to share their work through the lens of design. Though the group did not self-identify as designers, if educators and practitioners are interested in learning from diverse design methodologies, it makes sense to look beyond the boundaries of our professional discipline to find examples of successful design. In AfriCOBRA's work, we find a delightful use of expressive lettering, rhythmic patterns, and bold colors. This work is particularly inspiring because these artists found a way to codify their visual language. They decided on a shared aesthetic vision and executed it time and again. Working against the backdrop of the Civil Rights Movement, these artists intentionally pursued a Black aesthetic, reflecting pride in their community and identities.

As the article series grew, contributors began to submit essays about other design histories worthy of inclusion in the canon. Caspar Lam and YuJune Park wrote an essay about the Chinese Type Archive featuring the evolving typographic language of modern Chinese. Stephen Child and Isabella D'Agnenica contributed an article on the Gee's Bend Quilters, a group of Black women from Alabama who mastered an improvisational style of quilting. Dina Benbrahim wrote an essay titled "Moroccan Design Stories, with Shape and Soul," analyzing the typographic and geometric designs found within Moroccan design history. Other early contributors to the article series were Ali Place, who examined the role of women in computer programming, and Aggie Toppins, who investigated the story behind the I AM a Man placard from the 1968 Memphis sanitation workers' strike.

Now, as this work moves from an article series to a book, there is space for some of these essays to develop into fuller writings with more in-depth research. A critical component that I hope to achieve is to peel back the aesthetic layers of the designs to allow each reader to understand the social, political, and cultural contexts surrounding the making of the work. In examining the contexts, readers will discover how different cultural groups determine meaning, and how noncanonical ideologies and methods offer additional ways of making than what is offered by the grid-based Swiss styles of mainstream graphic design.

When I began this book process, I envisioned a neat and streamlined series of essays, matching in length and format. What developed over time became something much more organic, with essays and interviews of varying lengths. Often, I was left speechless and humbled at the generous sharing of knowledge. Nuveen Barwari's essay, "Kurdish Fragments: Mapping Pattern as Language," discusses the displacement of millions of Kurdish people and its impact on decorative art practices. She examines Kurdish rugs as artifacts of erasure, explaining how identity is employed through metaphors and floral themes. In my interview with Sadie Red Wing, she explains how Indigenous tribal communities have used Traditional Ecological Knowledge to inform their understanding of design and how visual sovereignty is at the heart of her work. In my conversation with Saki Mafundikwa, he explains how the colorful visual landscape of Zimbabwe offers a counter to the white space of German and Swiss design. He also draws comparisons between design and American soul music, bringing to light the creative genius of Black people across cultures and disciplines. Other essays and interviews in the book offer similar insight into perspectives and ideologies that aren't reflected in modernist design. Further still, design leaders Ellen Lupton and Cheryl D. Holmes Miller offer perspective on the future of design, its pedagogy, and ways to reconcile the past. Practitioners Tré Seals of Vocal Type and Zipeng Zhu discuss the relationship between their work and their identity.

This small sampling of stories offers more than a quick glimpse into design artifacts. It asks of the reader to consider what we don't know, and what questions have yet to be asked. It asks the reader to rethink the definition of design to expand beyond contemporary and digital practices and beyond the boundaries of the Western design canon.

GEE'S BEND QUILTERS

Stephen Child and Isabella D'Agnenica

ince the early 1900s, the women of Gee's Bend, Alabama, have narrated and rewritten their lives through the creation of quilts. While personally significant to the women, their families, and their community, the quilts have also been held up to artistic acclaim, in particular for their distinctive, brilliant designs. Comparisons of this unique aesthetic to the Bauhaus and other design movements have caused us to look again at the categories of art and craft, high art and folk art, and the value of art and who determines it. We explore here the historical context of the community that created these artists; the elements of their successful design aesthetic, particularly in comparison with the Western European canon; and the impact on the women and their work after being "discovered" by the art world.

The Life of Gee's Bend

Gee's Bend is a small, rural town in Wilcox County, Alabama, which sits enclosed on three sides by the Alabama River. It takes its name from a plantation owner, Joseph Gee, who settled the town and built his cotton plantation on the land in the early 1800s. With him, he brought a group of eighteen enslaved African Americans. After Gee's death, the plantation was sold to the Pettways, distant relatives of Gee, and then later sold to Adrian Sebastian Van de Graaff, a Tuscaloosa man who operated the plantation as an absentee landowner.[1]

After Emancipation, many of the formerly enslaved people became sharecroppers and tenant farmers. Already isolated and impoverished, conditions in Gee's

Bend became even worse in the early 1930s, when a merchant who had given credit to many of the community members passed away. Eager to collect on the debts, his family broke into the homes of Gee's Bend residents and forcibly took livestock, seeds, tools, and other possessions, leaving most people in the area with nothing. With few resources, the community was at one time considered one of the poorest communities in the entire United States, and the federal government stepped in. An article about the history of Gee's Bend summarizes this period:

> In 1937, the Van de Graaff family sold their land to the federal government, and the Farm Security Administration (FSA) established Gee's Bend Farms Inc., a pilot project of a cooperative program designed to sustain the inhabitants. The government built houses, subdivided the property, and sold tracts of land to the local families, for the first time giving the African American population control of the land they worked.[2]

While this government program did provide land to the community, economic circumstances remained harsh.

This history is significant because it was within this geographic, social, and economic context that women from Gee's Bend created a long and lasting quilting tradition. Quilts were originally created out of necessity. The women needed to keep themselves and their families warm but had little access to material. To solve this, they began recycling scraps of fabric from worn clothing and feed sacks. The results were bold both in color and in pattern. While some women made quilts that followed more "traditional" and ornate quilting patterns, many others began to deviate and create their own designs. In place of the quilting convention of small pieces of fabric pieced together with small stitches in repeating patterns, the women of Gee's Bend used larger, asymmetric shapes and more visible stitching.

The Quilters as Artists

In "'But a Quilt Is More': Recontextualizing the Discourse(s) of the Gee's Bend Quilts," Vanessa Kraemer Sohan rightly asks us to see the quilts as produced outside and within the boundaries of other quilting traditions, particularly other African American quilting traditions.[3] Gee's Bend quilts are distinct from the image that people might immediately conjure when they hear the word *quilt*, but as a group they share a similar aesthetic language, even among different quilters. This is what is particularly compelling about the Gee's Bend tradition—it is ever-evolving, growing from multiple traditions but always remade and re-formed by the individuals of each generation, as well as their respective circumstances.

Rather than follow traditional quilting patterns, most women made up the designs as they went along, creating what recent critics and art historians have dubbed an "improvisational" style of quilting.[4] Richard Kalina writes,

One of the things that makes ordinary quilts so likable is the way that they typically frame a wealth of detail in smallish, repeating patterns. You can look at a part of them and easily deduce the whole. There may be some framing devices, but essentially the pattern could repeat endlessly. The Gee's Bend quilts don't do that. They are bounded, unique, and rarely symmetrical. Even when symmetry is there, it is given a savvy, destabilizing push.[5]

While this shift away from symmetrical, repeating patterns may have begun out of a lack of materials and time, it continued and evolved through an aesthetic dialogue among the women in the community.

Women from Gee's Bend have spoken explicitly about how their quilting tradition has been passed down and elaborated on both from generation to generation and among community members. Mary Lee Bendolph remembered how she would take inspiration from other women's quilts: "I see other people's quilts like when the spring of the year comes. The women would hang their quilts out, and we would just go from house to house looking at the people's quilts. And I would take a pattern from looking at their quilt and try to make one like it."[6] This practice of artistic dialogue through observation and modification extended inside their homes, where women would showcase their quilts on beds and couches for company to see and to comment on quilts they found particularly beautiful.

The aesthetic dialogue that the women of Gee's Bend participated in can be viewed as similar in many

Mensie Lee Pettway, *Roman Stripes* variation with sashing, 1995, 89 x 71 in (226 x 180 cm). © 2023 Mensie Lee Pettway / Artists Rights Society (ARS), New York

ways to conversations by modernists around the same time relating to constructing and deconstructing grids in rhythmic and often unexpected ways.

The Gee's Bend Quilters were, and continue to be, collage artists. They worked with limited fabric swatches: leftover scraps from a piece of clothing that had just been made or pieces cut from clothing that was worn and ready to be discarded. They worked with what they had and turned it into meaningful and power-ful art. The grid structure, which was the compositional basis for most quilt making (then and now), provided a practical way for the disparate colors and patterns of the swatches to relate to one another and combine into a cohesive whole. Though now viewed as expres-sive, quilts were originally more practical in design. The women who made these quilts did not create them with the intention that they would be viewed in museums. They made them to keep their loved ones warm and to commemorate those who passed on. The narrowness of the choices in fabric and the formality of the grid structure contributes to the strength of the work. The artistry came from the expressive combinations of the swatches they put together.

Housetop, created by Nancy Pettway (b. 1935), is based on a three-column, four-row grid, with each section broken down into smaller and smaller concen-tric framelike subdivisions. The larger pieces frame the smaller ones around the center. This particular grid pattern and design can be traced back at least as far as 1830, with even deeper roots in African fractals and geometric relationships. In Pettway's improvisation, each grid section is a unique composition. While the various cloth pieces are held together by the grid, the framework is not rigid. The horizontal and vertical sections are not always cut straight and do not always line up with one another across the composition. This offset, where some sections stand firm while others are pushing up against one another, creates a jostling and swaying movement. This, in combination with the varying color and pattern, makes our eyes bounce around the elements without settling on one area for long. The making has an improvisational resonance and spontaneity that is masterful.

The square or rectangle is one of the most elemental shapes in the visual language, and Pettway plays with the simple shapes by contrasting their size (big and little), value (dark and light), color (hue and saturation), texture (floral patterns and flat), and orientation (horizontal and vertical). These opposites are what give the composition movement and rhythm. This piece is a kinesthetic symphony. The elements push, pull, and pulse with life, and this rhythm drives expression. We can hear the beat; we can taste the colors; we can feel the textures. The bright patterned or striped sections feel joyous and playful, but they are tempered with deep hues and worn sections that keep the piece grounded and help balance an overly sweet palette.

Comparisons of the Gee's Bend artists with European modernists are often made, and one can see why. Modernism asserted that simplicity and functionality were the keys to good design. The artists and designers of the Bauhaus, Germany's influential art school

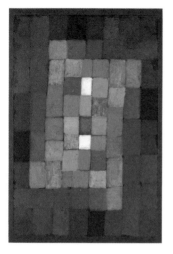

left: **Paul Klee, *Static-Dynamic Gradation*, 1923, oil and gouache on paper, bordered with gouache, watercolor, and ink, 15 x 10.25 in (38 x 26 cm). © 2022 Artists Rights Society (ARS), New York;** right: **Nancy Pettway, *Twelve-Block Variation on Housetop*, 2003, cotton and rayon, 86 x 76 in (218 x 193 cm). © 2022 Nancy Pettway / Artists Rights Society (ARS), New York**

(operational from 1919 to 1933), found expressive potential through simple geometric shapes. They pared down the visual vocabulary to its fundamental elements of line, circle, square, and triangle. They aimed to bring the fine and design arts into accord. The Bauhaus has been one of the most significant influences on design, and its impact is still being felt today. As the prominent Swiss designer Josef Müller-Brockmann has written, "The grid determines the constant dimensions of space. There's virtually no limit to the number of grid divisions. It may be said in general that every piece of work must be studied very carefully so as to arrive at the specific grid network corresponding to its requirements."[7] Graphic designers quickly realized the usefulness of using the grid as an organizing device.

Comparing a 1923 piece titled *Static-Dynamic Gradation* by the former Bauhaus teacher Paul Klee with Nancy Pettway's quilt reveals that they both used a grid structure as an organizing principle. Klee made numerous grid paintings and thought of his squares as musical notes that had a particular pitch and length of time within a signature. In this piece he carefully creates a glowing atmosphere from the dark desaturated colors on the outside to the light saturated colors in the center. He relies on analogous and complementary colors to create contrast and tension. Klee was a violinist and saw many analogies between his art and music. He wrote and spoke extensively about rhythm and movement in art.

Pettway's piece is as accomplished as any work by a modernist master. Klee's painting is controlled and modulated, while Pettway's composition includes unexpected anomalies. There are surprises everywhere. The heavy black bar at the bottom left of the quilt seems an odd choice, except she balances it with the darker strip that holds the right corner. The orange frame in the bottom center grid section jumps out strongly but is held in place and tempered by the orange pieces above and the beige swatches within. The quilt's composition is cohesive, and the irregularities provide a refreshing and striking orchestration.

In many ways, the Gee's Bend quilts share as many postmodern characteristics as they do features of modernism. The term *postmodernism* has caused controversy and is challenging because it holds various meanings in the world of art and design. It has often been a catch-all for concepts and styles that became widespread any time after modernism. There are several characteristics that we can point to, however, that suggest that Gee's Bend quilts should be viewed through this lens.

In a quilt called *Strip Quilt*, Arlonzia Pettway (1923–2008) used a wide variety of cloth sections. Besides a range of white, bright, and solid fabrics, there are also several striped, dotted, and checkered pieces of cloth. There are at least ten floral patterns thrown in the mix that come from different types of fabric with varying personalities. Pettway's bold composition of vertical stripes and the predominantly red, white, and mint-green palette keeps the diverse blend appealing.

Postmodernism design is similarly eclectic and fragmented, and it, too, plays with tradition. One can imagine Pettway choosing the various pieces at hand and laying out the composition. The process might seem rather random, but by cutting the pieces into relatively similar widths, she could move around the puzzle pieces so that the final arrangement vibrates with a syncopated rhythm.

To compare the quilters' work with European artistic theory or formal artistic perspectives helps amplify an understanding for some readers, but it can also get in the way of appreciating the quilts' unique expressions and significance. These are pieces by artists who were not trained in an art or design school or exposed to terms of Western art theory and vocabulary. They were not familiar with Klee's *Static-Dynamic Gradation* or Piet Mondrian's *Broadway Boogie Woogie*, but they operated within their own shared understanding of visual language. While each woman's work is distinct, their pieces are also members of the same aesthetic family.

What is significant about these quilts, in addition to their design artistry and aesthetic power, is how they reflect and have transformed the lives of the women who created them. They archive life.

In 1942 Missouri Pettway created a quilt out of her late husband's clothing. At a distance, the quilt consists of bold, irregular rectangles in muted grays, blues, reds, and whites. Small, diagonal stitches hold the pieces together, creating a subtle counterpattern. However, upon closer examination, rust stains and dirt, bleeding dye, and sun-bleached patches are visible. Pettway's daughter remembered the origins of the quilt: "Mama say, 'I going to take his work clothes, shape them into a quilt to remember him, and cover up under it for love.' She take his old pants legs and shirttails, take all the clothes he had, just enough to make that quilt."[8] Because of this labor of love, viewers can imagine the moments that might lead to each discoloration and mark. In addition to a stunning composition of abstract aesthetic relationship between colors and shapes, this quilt archives a narrative of Pettway and her husband's shared life.

The Mixed Blessing of Discovery

Circumstances for the women and recognition for their work changed dramatically in 1998, when the art historian and curator William Arnett ran across an image of a Gee's Bend woman named Annie Mae Young in a book on quilts. The image depicted Young next to a pile of logs covered by a quilt made up of denim patches with a red, yellow, and brown center. Arnett was enamored and headed to Wilcox County to find Young and her quilt. Arnett, who specialized in "vernacular" African American art, purchased Young's quilt for two thousand dollars (the average going rate for her quilts at that time was between five and fifteen dollars). This purchase began his relationship with the women of Gee's Bend and the emergence of their work in the "high" art arena. After his initial visit, Arnett went on to purchase an estimated seven hundred quilts over the years from the women of Gee's Bend. With these, he organized exhibitions at cultural institutions throughout the country, including the Milwaukee Art Museum, the Museum of Fine Arts Boston, and an extremely popular exhibition at the Whitney Museum of American Art.

These exhibitions situated Mary Lee Bendolph, Annie Mae Young, Loretta Pettway, and other Gee's Bend artists as discrete counterparts to European modernists like Henri Matisse and Klee, who also used bold color and abstraction in their work. Once in a museum context, the women's work was evaluated based on this new connection with "high" art and in relation to white male European modernists. The exhibitions also initiated conversations about the distinction between "art" and "craft." Alvia Wardlaw, curator and director of the University Museum at Texas Southern University, said, "The quilts reflect the history of [Gee's Bend] and of this country in their making and it asks all of us about genius…Where does it reside?"[9]

Installation view of *The Quilts of Gee's Bend* (Whitney Museum of American Art, New York, November 21, 2002–March 9, 2003). Left to right: Rachel Carey George, *Sixteen-Block Variation on Half-Log Cabin*, 1935; Annie Mae Young, *Medallion*, 1965; Jessie T. Pettway, *Bars and String-Pieced Columns*, 1950s. Photograph by Jerry L. Thompson. © Whitney Museum of American Art. Licensed by Scala / Art Resource, New York

These popular exhibitions brought much-deserved attention to the quilts and the women who created them. Reviewers, art historians, and visitors praised the improvisational style of the women's work, the bold color choices, and the deviation from traditional quilting while creating a new, shared aesthetic language and genre of quilting all their own.

These exhibitions, and the story of Gee's Bend quilters, also illuminate the fine (and sometimes not so fine) line between exposure and exploitation. The women's work was given a broad stage and has been celebrated throughout the United States and beyond as work of genius, thanks in large part to Arnett.

However, the financial profits gleaned from this recognition have not always filtered back to the women or the community of Gee's Bend. Images of the quilts have been reproduced on coffee mugs, calendars, scarves, and refrigerator magnets. The women's reactions to Arnett and others profiting from their work were mixed. While some women appreciated the recognition and the purchase of their work at far above the previous going rate, others were upset that people were profiting off their work without their consent. Loretta Pettway and Annie Mae Young both filed lawsuits against Arnett on the grounds that they had been cheated out of thousands of dollars in proceeds from their work and copyrights.

After winning various copyright disputes, an organization called X gained the rights to the work, ensuring that the Gee's Bend quilters receive proper compensation for the reproduction of their work. Today, the women of Gee's Bend continue to elaborate on their storied tradition. About forty women from the community are part of the Gee's Bend Quilting Collective, which is managed by Mary Ann Pettway and housed in a small building in town. Here, women continue to produce and sell quilts, often for up to one thousand dollars apiece. The collective also holds annual quilting retreats where participants can learn to quilt or practice their quilting skills with the guidance of Mary Ann Pettway and China Pettway.

In an essay about the Gee's Bend quilters, the social activist bell hooks wrote, "From the location of newly acquainted acclaim, they find a public voice to speak about the hardships they faced day to day, living as they say 'a starvation life' where everybody was just struggling to get by, to make a way out of no way. And yet in a life that was more often than not filled with hardship, pain, and sorrow, they found a pleasure of pleasure, of ecstasy, a place where they could transcend self, that place was artistic production—the making of quilts."[10] In addition to being aesthetically powerful, these quilts and the myriad stories behind them are important because they ask us to reconsider our aesthetic value system. Moreover, they serve as maps of an American history that is often unnarrated. These quilts were a way by which women in the community both reflected and transformed their material and social circumstances.

STEPHEN CHILD is chair of design and an associate professor of teaching at USC Iovine and Young Academy. Child has worked as a designer and art director in a wide variety of creative areas, including health care, entertainment, academe, and the nonprofit sector. He has worked at Dorlan+Sweeney Global Healthcare, Paramount Pictures, DZN the Design Group, 2G Studios, and BLT & Associates, among many others.

ISABELLA D'AGNENICA (BA in world arts and cultures, UCLA, 2020) creates documentaries, visual art, and scholarship to consider how our everyday social interactions are affected by documentation, media representation, and mythologies of the places in which we find ourselves. Isabella uses art making as a research modality and scholarly research as a basis for her art.

A CHINESE TYPOGRAPHIC ARCHIVE

Caspar Lam
and YuJune Park

Diagrams by Naiqian Wang and Stephanie Winarto

ver the past decade, Sinophone communities have seen a surge of interest in Chinese typography. A new generation of practitioners is trying to reconcile the tradition of one of the world's oldest written languages with the practice of graphic design in a pluralistic and multicultural context.

The form of written Chinese has a lineage stretching back to the first inscriptions used for divination in the second millennium BCE. The vast distance of time and memory traversed between those first oracle bones and the present day covers all manner of printing technologies and cultural encounters that make this area of design simultaneously exciting and also thoroughly overwhelming.

Recent Memories of Modern Chinese

Today's written Chinese is the result of its interactions with modernity. Closely coupled with but not entirely synonymous with Westernization, modernity is an elusive concept. It can be seen as causal reactions to encounters with foreign powers, particularly but not exclusively the West; the 1912 fall of the Qing, China's last imperial dynasty; the emergence of Republican and later Communist governments; the transfer of technologies like letterpress; and increasing industrialization and urbanization. Chinese modernization can also be seen as the alteration and even disruption of a Sinocentric cultural narrative that had to accommodate the national experiences of the nineteenth and twentieth centuries. One might even say that the adoption of the Gregorian calendar in 1912 by the Chinese Republican government marked the beginning of a new, modern time. These changes are reflected in the Chinese language, not only on a linguistic but also on a graphic level, and were tied to larger notions of nationalism and literacy. The process of modernization has affected everything that graphic designers might see as language made materially visible. Broadly speaking, the changes to the Chinese language could be summed up in shifting ideas about unification, vernacularization, simplification, and romanization.

Up until the twentieth century, texts were written in Classical Chinese, a terse, formal style of writing that differed in syntax and style from spoken Chinese. In this context, spoken Chinese, too, differed from locale to locale, with wide variations in pronunciation and modulations in expression. Phonologically, China was and continues to be diverse, even though those differing sounds share the same written form. This is to say, sound and script are generally divorced. After the fall of the Qing Dynasty, there was a concerted push to adopt a national spoken language and, in parallel, to use vernacular syntax in writing. Simply, this meant that the patterns of writing would follow the patterns of everyday speech, in this case, Mandarin Chinese. Vernacularization also coincided with the emergence and adoption of standardized punctuation, since histori-cally, Classical Chinese did not use punctuation. For many Chinese, the use of a standard dialect and accessi-ble writing style served practical aims of unifying the country as well as increasing literacy.

華

Character for **brilliance/ magnificence**

China

Beijing

Shanghai

Guangzhou

huá

Pronunciation in
Mandarin
Pinyin Transliteration

gho

Pronunciation in
Wu
Common Wu Pinyin
Transliteration

waa4

Pronunciation in
Cantonese
Jyutping Transliteration

Traditional Chinese

白駒食場。

鳴鳳在樹，

Simplified Chinese

鸣凤在树，

白驹食场。

top: **Chinese topolects pronounce the same character differently.**
bottom: **Simplified Chinese reduces the number of strokes in many
traditional Chinese characters. Additionally, simplified Chinese is
usually read horizontally from left to right, while traditional Chinese
is historically read vertically from right to left.**

Language reform did not end there. Proposals abounded for the script itself, viewed by some with pride and others as a problem that contributed to China's inability to participate effectively on the world stage. Some advocated replacing the script, which comprised tens of thousands of characters, with the twenty-six letters of the Roman alphabet tied to particular spoken sounds of Chinese. Others suggested abandoning Chinese altogether in favor of an international auxiliary language like Esperanto. A less radical change was stroke simplification from traditional to simplified Chinese, which was adopted in 1956 in mainland China. Simplification meant a reduction of the number of strokes needed to write a character, which in theory would speed up writing, ease language learning, and increase literacy. The directionality of writing also shifted, too, from a vertical right-left orientation to a horizontal left-right orientation.

For a language as old as Chinese, some of its visual grammar is therefore, paradoxically, quite new; these changes are still within living memory for Sinophone communities. Indeed, modernization is not something that occurred but that continues to occur. A quick look at any Chinese calendar in screen or print will reveal the persistence of the old lunar calendar living on as annotations of solar time, reflecting a Chinese tendency for ancient customs and new ideas to coexist in a variety of configurations. In language, vestiges of Classical Chinese appear in formalized settings; countless varieties of Chinese topolects like Cantonese continue to exist alongside Mandarin; and romanization schemes like pinyin have assumed the role of phoneticization to mediate among Chinese, other languages, and technologies like the keyboard. Finally, traditional Chinese remains in use in places like Hong Kong, Taiwan, and diasporic communities, while simplified Chinese enjoys currency in mainland China, Singapore, and other international contexts. It is within this complexity that graphic designers have to maneuver to find space for both reverence and revelry.

The Visual Mechanics of Chinese

This tendency for accrual is paralleled in the visual structure of the Chinese script. A closer look at Chinese and its typographic forms will quickly reveal a recurring tension with scale and modular complexity. Written Chinese is a historical collection of characters embodying a multiplicity of ideas developed over four millennia. Both Chinese and non-Chinese commentators often unduly emphasize the pictographic origins of Chinese. In practice, the number of these characters are dwarfed by the vast majority of characters that signify sound and meaning. Like a compound word in English, a single Chinese character can be the result of multiple lexical units remixed and recombined in not only one but two dimensions to form today's eighty-thousand-plus standard and variant characters (although in practice, less than ten thousand are in use).

Historically, the combinatorics enabled by the modular structure of Chinese has led to constant growth in the inventory of characters, despite periodic attempts at pruning by ruling authorities. It should also be noted

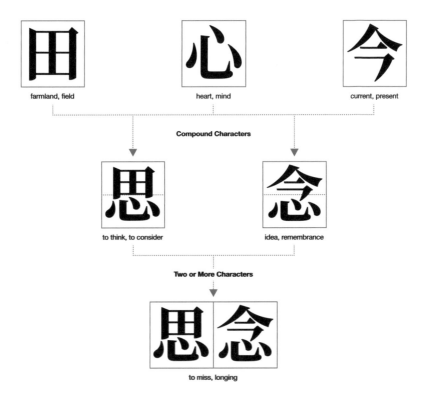

A word can be made from...
Single Component Characters

田
farmland, field

心
heart, mind

今
current, present

Compound Characters

思
to think, to consider

念
idea, remembrance

Two or More Characters

思念
to miss, longing

The relationship among parts of a character, a character, and a word can be complex. Many characters are composed of smaller parts derived from other characters, and one or more characters can denote a word.

that a single character does not share cardinality with a single word: that is, one, two, or more characters can mean a word. Graphically, Chinese could be seen reductively, on the one hand, as a series of modules nested within the squarish boundary of the character and expansively, on the other hand, as the tiling of characters form larger compositional blocks. Predictably, the squarish modularity of the character exerts its outward influence on the grid of the page. The page obeys the character, not the other way around. Thus Chinese texts tend to be justified, with alphabetic interlopers having to accommodate to this regularity through their own kerning adjustments.

Though the square boundary of the character provides a useful compositional shorthand, the character's self-contained visual unit is defined less by obedience to this boundary than by a defined order of strokes radiating from an invisible center of gravity. There is no baseline on which characters sit. They hang in space and contribute to the adaptability for Chinese to both vertical and horizontal reading. Hence, Chinese readers were already visually primed for the twentieth-century switch from vertical to horizontal reading orientations, though traditionalists will emphasize the overall downward physiognomy of Chinese characters, expressed through stroke order and composition. In everyday life, characters are frequently seen running downward, rightward, leftward, and even—on a crowded streetscape—turning corners.

Held together by the center of gravity, the nested modules within a character have provided the

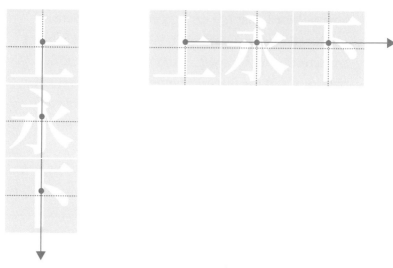

The center of gravity is the point from which a character radiates out. It acts as a baseline and allows characters to be read vertically and horizontally.

conditions for the appearance of new and nonstandard characters, visual puns, and graphic play. For graphic designers, a common trope includes replacing parts of a character with images to create rebus-like forms that blur the distinctions between type, symbol, and image. Such techniques were common in lettering of the twentieth century and continue today, particularly in design exercises involving Chinese type. In fact, the modular and logical nature of Chinese has allowed an almost limitless ability for the script to reconfigure itself and with it an expansion of scale that dwarfs other languages. It is this characteristic that has defined the language's interactions with print technology and, in turn, graphic design.

Chinese Print Technology and Typefaces

Up until the twentieth century, most books were produced with comparatively inexpensive woodblock printing rather than with available movable type technology. Although the Chinese invented and experimented with movable type materials like clay, wood, and metal, it was Western missionaries in the nineteenth century who made concerted efforts to develop lead movable type for Western-style printing presses. Early letters from Western missionaries devoted a fair amount of time discussing the costs needed to create such movable metal type in Chinese. These concerns echo events in Chinese print history like the melting of metal type in the imperial palace because of a coinage shortage in the eighteenth century.

Aside from the price of materials and labor in producing metal type, movable type of any material is only cost-efficient if efforts like retrieving and organizing type are factored into the mix for each print run. While this is negligible for an alphabetic script, retrieving and organizing type for a character-based script like Chinese requires a skilled and educated labor force. In the Chinese context, woodblock printing was simply a far more economical option for most print purposes. More important, it aligned with the material and aesthetic ecosystem in China. Woodblock printing not only used the same water-based inks used for calligraphy but also re-created its effects. When compared with the stiff attempts of Europeans to create Chinese type, it is not surprising that Western print technologies and their associated typefaces did not perform favorably when they were first introduced in the early nineteenth century. It was only later in the nineteenth century and into the twentieth that a confluence of war, industrial capitalism, newer print technologies like electrotyping, and the transference of this print technology into the hands of the Chinese that allowed movable metal type to take root. Still, the business of making type continued to be a difficult undertaking, with typefaces being produced primarily within large, well-funded publishing-printing houses.

The dearth of metal movable type did not mean that printed type did not exist in China prior to the eighteenth century. Four typeface families are commonly recognized as having emerged over the long course of Chinese print history since Bi Sheng's invention of movable type during the eleventh century: Regular Script, Songti, Imitation Song, and Heiti. In brief, Regular Script is a calligraphic style that matured in the Tang Dynasty and was also used in print contexts. Its stroke order and appearance continue to define the standardized shape of Chinese. Originating in the Song but maturing in the Ming Dynasty, Songti departs from Regular Script in its rectilinear appearance. Its thick verticals and thin horizontals terminate in characteristically triangular forms and are associated with the printed appearance of texts. Imitation Song emerged as a revival in the early twentieth century and reintroduced the slant of the hand in Songti typefaces. Finally, Hei-style typefaces are a Japanese import of the 1930s; they are derivations of grotesque European typefaces.

Regular Script

Based on a basic brush script, Regular Script has angled horizontal strokes and soft terminals.

Songti

Songti strokes end in triangular terminals based on the pools of ink at the end of a stroke. Horizontal strokes are always straight.

Imitation Song

A hybrid of Regular Script and Songti, horizontal strokes in Imitation Song are tilted, and strokes have less exaggerated terminals.

Heiti

Less lineweight variation occurs in Heiti. Terminals have flat endings and may be flared outward on both sides.

The four main Chinese typeface families: Regular Script, Songti, Imitation Song, and Heiti.

Examples of meishuzi for the phrase meaning "Chinese style" from *Zhongxi wanyou meishuzi* **(Chinese and Western Meishuzi), edited by Shi Peiqing, 1948.**

In addition to these broad categories of type, there is also a distinct tradition of display lettering called meishuzi, used predominantly for signage and display purposes, which proliferated between the 1920s and 1970s. Treating type through the lens of image making, early meishuzi experimented with boisterous forms that pushed the boundaries of legibility before settling into the more recognizable habitus of Chinese type by the mid-twentieth century. Meishuzi, then, along with printed type and Chinese calligraphy, form the triumvirate on which much of today's Chinese typographic discourse is based.

Rectifying Names and Being on the Same Page

Against the backdrop of global typography, it is clear that Chinese type history does not fall neatly into the relationships of materials and techniques that arose in European print history. Though invented in China, movable type's impact on China was not an inflection point as it was in Europe. Up until the twentieth century, woodblock printing continued to be the predominant form of printing. Even within the technology of movable type, wood was preferred over metal. This meant that each character was individually carved, which raises questions about the nature of type as a set of repeating, duplicated forms. Finally, calligraphy has continued to actively exert an influence on the Chinese aesthetic imagination. These factors lead to the inevitable conclusion that an alphabetic concept of typography may be subject to reconfiguration.

With no shortage of vantage points from which to parse the complexity of Chinese, all of the usual factors of historicism, nationalism, technological positivism, and pure pragmatics are at play when so many stakeholders and actors spread across the world are involved. But before such paths are explored, a corpus of forms is needed from which these comparisons and arguments can be made. Despite—or perhaps because of—China's long tradition of calligraphy, typography has not historically been viewed as a craft worthy of attention in Chinese culture. In historical printed forms, references will be made to the printed samples of a particular printer, but there are generally *no specific names* to describe the typefaces in question.

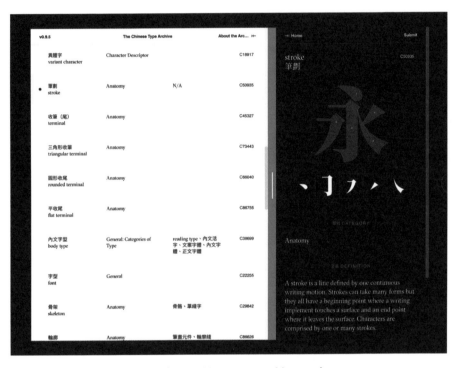

The Chinese Type Archive (www.chinesetypearchive.com).

In addition, China's vast linguistic, geographic, and temporal diversity means that familiar things might be described in subtly shaded ways. A case in point: Songti has also been referred to historically as hard type, square type, or even craftsmen-style type. In this way, the vocabulary used to describe typography and design is a game of telephone from the past and through other cultures like Japan, from which twentieth-century Chinese artisans imported many ideas and terms like *design lettering* and *commercial lettering*. Without nominal markers and synonyms, even if imprecise, it becomes significantly more difficult to compare, theorize, and critique. This becomes compounded when trying to situate Chinese typography in a globalized context.

Building an Evolving Database of Chinese Typography

It is in this context that an accessible and open database was needed to support and allow distinct perspectives on the growth and evolution of Chinese type. Simply put: Where could one find a list of Chinese typefaces, books, and typographic terms? This deceptively simple question gave rise to an ongoing, collaborative, open-access index of Chinese typographic resources: the Chinese Type Archive (www.chinesetypearchive.com).

Within the database, three main sections—resources, typefaces, and concepts—catalog key information that allows designers, students, and educators to jump-start their investigations into Chinese type. Each resource record is linked, where possible, to OCLC's WorldCat to allow users to find that item in the user's local library. Typeface and concept records capture different names and synonyms that reveal how these artifacts and ideas have changed over time. To make this possible, each record is given a unique identifier that is stable and never changes. This resolves a key challenge in typographic discourse: as collective understanding of Chinese typography changes and grows, the Chinese Type Archive can capture these shifts and update these records while ensuring that they remain findable and linkable. Discernible changes in the way Chinese typographic vocabulary is deployed and standardized has already occurred in the past decade. Seeing this happen in real time is a rare and exciting opportunity.

At present, the archive contains over eight hundred typefaces, concepts, and resources, with more continuing to be submitted by the public and added by a dedicated community of volunteers and research assistants who find and cross-reference entries and draw diagrams. As the archive grows, images will be added in addition to new functional enhancements to the site. Educators using the site will immediately notice that the entire site is bilingual, which is part of a broader aim to build bridges between Chinese typography and the wider typographic community. As more records are created, it will become easier to find points of similarity and difference among these systems that can serve to enrich design pedagogy at large. In addition, as an open access resource, the data are making their way into other websites like the popular Fonts In Use site to support the general design community.

Learning through Collecting

The growing corpus of ideas and forms within the Chinese Type Archive begins to offer a space where a multiplicity of interpretations can exist in order to thread together the many shifts in the Chinese script and their aesthetic ramifications. Because such shifts are still within living memory of many Sinophone communities and are evolving in parallel to China's role on the world stage, it is essential to capture the many facets of these aesthetic conversations—emerging typography, changing definitions, and new literature— which often end up brushing against contentious issues of cultural and national identity. Contrary to what many in and outside China may think, Chinese type is not one monolithic block.

The act of collecting, then, is the flip side of making. Precedents give designers the ability to build on or react against previous decisions. In this act of collecting, particularly in the area of typography, definitional questions about the field are instantiated into the structure of the catalog, in the determination of what to collect and how to organize and describe what has been collected. In the case of Chinese type, the simple practice of collecting complete specimens belies the inherent inadequacies of current conceptions of type. For instance, most designers assume that a typeface is "complete" when it contains all the glyphs needed to compose every possible word. By this definition, most, if not all, Chinese typefaces are not complete. In another example, most designers have a mental model of lead type or a set of digital type as a typographic product. Given that the Chinese historically experimented with type outside these categories, how should one define artifacts like stamps and woodblocks that may fall outside the realm of type in a European context? The challenge of teasing out these distinctions, then, begins to refine the contours of typography.

Takeaways

Technology, culture, and politics influence aesthetic form. Interrogating design tools and the socioeconomic conditions that enable these methods of production allows designers to situate their present work in relation to works from the past.

Consider the similarities and differences between Chinese and Latin typographic concepts. Note how design systems respond differently when confronted with different levels of scale and complexity.

Collecting is the flip side of making. Collections are repositories with generative potential for a multiplicity of stories and lines of thought. This simple act is a way to understand the breadth of material, to ascertain precedents, and to allow others to partake and draw their own conclusions.

CASPAR LAM is a designer and strategist experienced with solving information-driven challenges for the cultural heritage, education, and technology sectors. He is a partner at Synoptic Office, an assistant professor of communication design at Parsons School of Design, and the program director of its BFA Communication Design program.

YUJUNE PARK is a designer and educator with deep expertise in strategy, branding, hybrid physical-digital experiences, and the cultural heritage sector. She is a partner at Synoptic Office and an associate professor of communication design at Parsons School of Design where she has served as program director.

INDIGENOUS SOVEREIGNTY and DESIGN

An Interview with
Sadie Red Wing
(Her Shawl Is Yellow)

I find myself in a position to be a historian. I never thought I would be, but I have to be a historian in order to bring more Indigenous people into the classrooms. It's a fight to preserve history. A lot of that comes from a focus on strategy, reciprocity, longevity, and sustainability. Since Eurocentric or Western histories don't document for the Indigenous people, there is a fight for inclusivity.

—*Sadie Red Wing*

Sadie Red Wing is an Indigenous design educator representing the Lakȟóta/Dakȟóta tribe. She is a fierce advocate for tribal visual sovereignty in her research and design work. When I sat down with Sadie, she talked to me about tribal values, Traditional Ecological Knowledge, and what the design industry can learn from Indigenous people.

What We Need to Know

While the design industry has made increased efforts in recent years to be more inclusive of Indigenous people, there is still a great deal to learn about the noncolonial values and methods that make up their design history. "There's a lot of expertise in Indigenous tribal culture that demonstrates very strategic design practices. We're very fortunate to know what a tribe is. So, when you want to talk about community, organization, and designing systems, I see that in the realm of design." Sadie noted that many traditional Americans, Canadians, and Mexicans may have difficulty understanding tribal values because of colonialism's emphasis

The Buffalo Nation Will Rise Again, poster, 17 x 11 in (43 x 28 cm)
Before Western colonization, the Pté Oyáte, or Buffalo Nation, roamed the Great Plains in the United States. Lakȟóta/Dakȟóta tribes viewed the buffalo as a close relative that provided resources to survive, like food, textiles, tools, shelter, ceremonial objects, protection, migration patterns, and cultural knowledge that demonstrates values of reciprocity.
—Sadie Red Wing, "Pte Oyate"

on individualism rather than community. She notes that her perspective within design is community-based, because that is how a tribe functions. She added that one of the key values within a tribal community is a focus on reciprocity, an idea intricately tied to Indigenous lifestyle that is lacking in many design practices. "The reciprocal concept that you're missing in design, or in a function, or in a system, is having a responsibility that demonstrates a task, and that task helps function the society to keep working for hundreds and hundreds and hundreds of years." She gave examples of the ways in which we see reciprocity on display in nature, and its connection to sustainability.

> We see how trees clean the air. We see how bees pollinate. There are a lot of metaphors, I guess, related to land. If I'm coming in and I'm talking about civic engagement, designing systems, or community building aspects, I'm going to ask how it can be done organically. How can it be done with human energy? How can it be done to keep society going? So, when we start to talk about Indigeneity, now we're talking about a reciprocal cycle of taking care of the lands.

Before going further, Sadie made the distinction between *Indigenous* and *Native American*. She explained that the two terms are not necessarily inter-changeable. Indigenous can describe any person that comes from a history that relates to a place and who is invested in keeping that place alive: "When we say the word *Indigenous*, we're talking about anybody that has a history rooted to land—it doesn't matter where it is. It could be in Africa, Australia, the Antarctic... the Amazon. We all have those same tasks and responsibility of reciprocity."

Learning Design from Nomadic Prairie Life

Sadie underscored the complexity of interrelated experiences that need to be acknowledged before anyone can begin to understand visual sovereignty or decolonization. For the Indigenous, the visual and cultural values of a place are influenced by the physical terrain and the associated responsibility of caring for that land. "You have to know that I come from the prairie. I don't come from the desert. I don't come from the Atlantic or the Pacific coast. I don't come from the very tundra Antarctic area. I'm coming in from the prairie." She commented that many people do not know what the United States looked like precolonization, making it difficult for some to visualize the grasslands, and added, "I'm coming in as an expert as a nomad. I can't live that lifestyle now, the way that the United States or Canada is run. But, that's how the world makes sense for me." Sadie explained that nomadic Indigenous people have a long history with a lot of expertise surrounding how to take care of the land. However, much of what is learned is not from reading it in textbooks but through Traditional Ecological Knowledge.

When you're nomadic, the goal is so simple that it's overlooked. Everything that is ingrained in my

DNA is to make sure that grass grows. How are you going to make it grow? Strategy. We knew that we needed buffalo because buffalo are the perfect weight. They're heavy and they have little feet, but they are also quick. So by following and studying the buffalo we learned how to keep grass growing. We learned that we needed the weight of the buffalo, and their feet, because we didn't have machines or tractors. We didn't have it, but we also didn't need it. They're not staying in one place and continuing to stomp on the same soil. They have a large migration pattern because of their size. So if you can envision the United States being predominantly prairie, then you'd have greater respect for how that huge creature did a lot of tilling. The challenge is, Traditional Ecological Knowledge is not preserved the same way as other knowledge is preserved. So think of the buffalo as my printing press. That's my tool. That's all I know.

Sustainability

Sadie then elaborated a bit more on the use of tools and the connection to a value system tied to sustainability. She noted that despite the success of the printing press, it has its drawbacks, including Europeans' overuse of paper as a primary resource. "You're gonna need paper for binding elements. You're going to need it to print Bibles, currency, flyers, and more." Still, even given that exploitation of materials, she applauded the strategy of using the press as a communication tool.

The Europeans were really good at documenting and preserving history with that printing press. That invention allowed them to make books faster. More books equals more bookshelves. More bookshelves equal more libraries. There's all the design elements of preservation...One of the reasons why the printing press is such a really good design is because it was invented for mass communication and multiple reproduction. That concept of mass reproduction or mass media is very powerful.

Sadie noted that a nomadic lifestyle would not allow for a machine that requires staying in one place or carrying heavy materials like metal.

What do typographers do? They reinvent different ways to change those twenty-six letters. So, I'm thinking about material things. You've got the bold *B*, the tiny *b*, the slanted *B*, and the sans serif *B*. Now you're just accumulating more and more stuff. I don't think people realize that when you have words that go from ten letters long to thirty letters long and you're expected to write an essay and your essays get longer and longer and longer...that's just more stuff. As a nomad, I'm just taking what I need with me. And so, when you start to think about "Why did you guys live in teepees? Why did you make clothing out of buffalo hide? Why wouldn't you trade for silk to get more cotton?" It's because we're on the move. The buffalo don't wait for nobody. So yes, the printing press is probably a good invention, but it wasn't needed over here. When you ask me, "Why don't you have your own libraries? Why don't you have your own archives, or your own website?" it's because it's kind of wasteful for us. When you look at the practice of graphic design, it's a profession where you stay put and your inventions are the ones that do all the work for you. For us, it's the opposite, because we're constantly on the go. So, when you understand those values, then you'll understand why Indigenous people have more symbol-based forms of recording.

Visual Language

Our conversation shifted to the use of symbols as visual communication:

> If I'm talking about the importance of buffalo and how we need the buffalo and the sun to grow flowers, I don't need to type you a thirty-four-page essay to do that. I'm probably gonna write a symbol instead. This gets into semiotics. With a logo, you can remember something based on a color, or a scent, even in a little tiny image. So, we have strong histories that are documented and symbol-based. When we get into the conventions of how some of these symbols look patternlike, you see that a lot of those pattern forms come from our beliefs of reciprocity and balance. It is a strategy to use a symbol as a memory device or a recording cue.

She explained that balance and symmetry are strong values that are often demonstrated as reflection in tribal symbols. Going back to what's learned through Traditional Ecological Knowledge and nomadic lifestyle, Sadie gave examples of how someone could learn the concept of balance by observing nature. "I didn't need a textbook to show what symmetry looked like… If you look at beautiful flowers on the water, then you would know." She adds, "Let's say that the Lakȟótas are gonna go visit the Mayans, and we didn't have horses yet. In the canoe ride, I'm looking down and seeing my reflection in the water. If I'm seeing other canoes, I can see the reflection on the water. That's our image of where symmetry comes from."

Goals

Throughout our conversation, what became apparent was that all of Sadie's work is connected to her tribal responsibilities. Her role as an educator and advocate for Indigenous visual sovereignty is deeply rooted and focused on the future of her community.

> I find myself in a position to be a historian. I never thought I would be, but I have to be a historian in order to bring more Indigenous people into the classrooms. It's a fight to preserve history. A lot of that comes from a focus on strategy, reciprocity, longevity, and sustainability. Since Eurocentric or Western histories don't document for the Indigenous people, there is a fight for inclusivity.

When Sadie talks about design, she says that she is not necessarily talking about visual culture. She's discussing how purpose, tasks, and responsibility go into how Indigenous people make clothes, food, and all other elements of culture. It's only then that you can understand sovereignty.

If I have to prepare students to go back to a reservation or go back to their sovereign nation, and if you don't understand what sovereignty is in the United States, you're not going to understand why my curriculum is so important. We need educated people to go work at tribal governments... I'm not here to come in and challenge anybody at the end of the day. So if my main goal is to get more tribal members to work at the Spirit Lake Dakota Nation Government, how do we show our sovereignty? And if you don't know our sovereignty, how can I help design something that shows the almost six hundred mini countries in the United States? What can I design for you that's going to allow that? One of the strongest tools is a map. If a map helps you identify countries, then we're going to need some better maps. Who's teaching somebody to design maps? That's my main goal. At the end of the day, it's about my people."

SADIE RED WING (HER SHAWL IS YELLOW)
is an Indigenous design educator whose work is centered around visual sovereignty for tribal nations. Sadie currently teaches at OCAD University in Toronto, Canada.

HOMELAND and LIFE: The Consequences of the Iconic Imagery of the Cuban Revolution

Elaine Lopez

In 1970 Susan Sontag wrote one of the most eloquent and detailed essays about the poster. This 14,133-word essay, titled "Posters: Advertisement, Art, Political Artifact, Commodity," was first published in Dugald Stermer's *The Art of Revolution: 96 Posters from Cuba*.[1] This oversize book features the essay in Spanish and full-size reproductions of iconic posters created during the revolution. Sontag goes into the fascinating origins of posters, their evolution, and their use across cultures. She then praises the uniqueness of the OSPAAAL (Organization of Solidarity with the People of Asia, Africa and Latin America) posters for being created outside the capitalist system and for their goal of inspiring and demonstrating solidarity.

I came across this essay during a graduate seminar in the first year of my MFA at RISD. At first, I was thrilled. Until this point, there had been few references to Cuban culture throughout my education, and I was so excited to learn about the intersection of design and Cuba. However, as the piece began blindly praising the revolutionary government, I recognized it for the propaganda that it was. My grandfather had been a political prisoner for six years—eventually leading our family to seek asylum in the United States to escape further persecution and hardship. It was jarring to see the cause of so much family trauma praised in the context of academe. (I later experienced this many more times.) The classroom discussion of the piece was equally disappointing, as it focused mostly on the aesthetic qualities of the posters instead of the implications.

What did I expect? Many barely understand US history, let alone the intricacies of geopolitics. As we expand the canon to include a broader range of works, we risk misrepresenting their origins, creators, or the current context. It is important to be thorough and sensitive about historical artifacts and to make space for students to share their perspectives—if they feel comfortable doing so.

• • •

July 11, 2022, marks the first anniversary of the largest Cuban antigovernment demonstrations seen in a generation, triggered by the growing scarcity of food, resources, and medicine caused by the COVID-19 pandemic. These protests were remarkable because they showed Cuban citizens publicly expressing their frustration with the lack of civil liberties under the authoritarian rule of the Communist government.

In Cuba, peaceful assembly for protest is technically legal according to the Cuban constitution, but this right is denied by authorities.[2] As a result, Cuba currently ranks sixth worldwide for most people incarcerated per capita.[3] These facts may seem surprising to those who view Cuba as a beacon of revolution and socialist ideals. This disjunction between reality and the projected narrative is due in part to the successful propaganda of the Cuban Revolution and government. Much of this propaganda has been graphic: iconic portraits, colorful posters, and captivating films, all worthy of inclusion in the global design canon. However, it is critical to understand the context behind these works before blindly celebrating their aesthetic qualities. This essay gives historical context to the most iconic design pieces from the Cuban Revolution and provides examples of critical contemporary works that reflect the current struggle for freedom.

Guerrerillo Heroico

Graphics have long served to seduce and distract the public from the real issues in the country. The most ubiquitous example of Cuban propaganda is the iconic portrait of Che Guevara that can be seen on T-shirts and souvenirs worldwide, used to represent the very idea of revolution. While this image is instantly recognizable, very few people outside the island understand its origins and the complexities of the politics that it represents.

While working as a photojournalist for the newspaper *Revolucion*, Alberto Korda took the portrait of Che Guevara on March 4, 1960, at a memorial service for the victims of the explosion of the French freighter *La Coubre*. It was during this memorial that Fidel Castro gave the speech where he first used the words *Patria o Muerte* (homeland or death). The image, later titled *Guerrerillo Heroico* (heroic guerrilla fighter), was not used for the article about the explosion and remained relatively obscure until Guevara's assassination in 1967. Upon hearing of his death, Korda gave the portrait to José Gómez Fresquet, a designer, who printed the image on red paper to create a poster for the memorial. The portrait was then printed on a five-story banner draped

Portrait of Ernesto "Che" Guevara.

over the Ministry of the Interior in the Plaza de la Revolucion to serve as a backdrop for Guevara's eulogy, which Castro delivered to one million mourners. The image remains there now, cast in permanent steel as an outline of the portrait.

While this image was revered by those who supported the revolution and communist causes in Cuba and worldwide, it also elicits adverse reactions in those affected negatively by the revolution and the specific policies created by Che Guevara. By the time of Guevara's death in 1967, half a million Cubans had fled the island. They fled for many reasons, including political and religious persecution and economic instability. Cubans who identified as homosexual or who did not fit into the revolution's rigid and traditional gender roles were targeted as social deviants. *In Cuba: An American History*, Ada Ferrer writes:

> They were purged from the university and other institutions, barred membership in the Communist Party, and generally condemned as standing outside of the revolution. In 1965, the government opened camps in the countryside where gays—and others deemed "anti-social"—would be rehabilitated as "new men."...Run by the military, with social workers and psychologists on staff, they combined forced labor with such practices as hormone and talk therapy.[4]

For those who experienced and fled this oppressive regime, this image—found worldwide—is a reminder of the trauma and loss they experienced during this time.

OSPAAAL Posters

Guerrerillo Heroico is present in many posters created by OSPAAAL, a political movement formed at the First Tricontinental Conference in Havana in 1966, and sponsored by the Cuban government. This conference brought together delegates from national liberation movements and political parties from Africa, Asia, and Latin America to discuss anticolonialism worldwide.[5] Through their conversations, they identified that it would be essential to design promotional materials to disseminate their message of solidarity.

One of OSPAAAL's primary methods of communication was a quarterly magazine titled *Tricontinental*. From its inception in 1967, *Tricontinental* included propaganda posters. These flat, bold, psychedelic screen-printed posters effectively use graphics to bring

Installation view of *Designed in Cuba: Cold War Graphics*, exhibition at the House of Illustrations, King's Cross, London, 2019–20.

RETALIATION TO CRIME: REVOLUTIONARY VIOLENCE
REPONSE AU CRIME: LA VIOLENCE RÉVOLUTIONNAIRE
RESPUESTA AL ASESINATO: VIOLENCIA REVOLUCIONARIA

Lithographic poster published by OSPAAAL.

attention to complex issues like racism, inequity, and colonization. Their eclectic appearance is owed to the variety of artists, art directors, and designers who contributed to this project throughout the years the magazine was in print. Artists were granted stylistic freedom when creating the posters, allowing them to experiment and apply aesthetic styles of the time. Influences from the Pop Art movement and the works of Milton Glaser and Andy Warhol are evident. In their effort to reach a global audience and practice accessibility, the text on the posters was often in multiple languages—English, French, Spanish, and Arabic. The content of many of the early posters focused on the announcement of days of solidarity with various causes and people around the world—Zimbabwe, Vietnam, Korea, Latin America, and Mozambique. Others declared solidarity with African Americans and the Black Power Movement, often borrowing and remixing the work of Emory Douglas (minister of culture and designer for the Black Panther Party) with his permission.

NOW!

One poster, designed in black and white, features the word *NOW!* set in a large, bold, condensed typeface that takes up half the page. Beneath the type is a watercolor illustration of a white police officer pushing back a young Black man with his left hand and holding a baton in his right hand. This poster references the 1965 film titled *NOW!*, by Santiago Álvarez.[6] Some consider this short film (5:21) to be one of the first examples of a music video. Found documentary footage of police brutality in the United States is expertly collaged and accompanied by a haunting song by Lena Horne set to the tune of "Hava Nagila"—a subtle hint meant to evoke the connection between racism in the United States and Nazi Germany. The song calls for equality and an end to racial discrimination.

Unfortunately, this video and song remain as relevant as ever—as police brutality continues across the United States. While the intent and message of these posters and films are urgent, valid, and worthy of inclusion in the design canon, it is essential to note that they served a political purpose for Cuba's revolutionary government. By focusing on issues in the United States, they attempted to deflect attention from the racism and violence that occurs on the island against its dissidents. There are countless examples on the Internet of Cuban police officers brutally beating unarmed citizens for speaking out against the government, demanding the release of political prisoners, and disagreeing with oppressive policies.

Patria y Vida

Another, more recent song and music video have become the Cuban rallying cry for freedom. "Patria y Vida," by Yotuel, Descemer Bueno, Gente de Zona, Maykel Osorbo, and El Funky, was released on February 16, 2021. Its title reclaims the phrase *Patria o Muerte* (homeland or death). *Patria y Vida* translates as "homeland and life." The lyrics call for freedom from the stale doctrines of the Cuban Revolution. They refer to the time that has passed since the revolution by repeating, "You're fifty-nine" (as in 1959), "I'm double two's" (as in 2020), and "sixty years of stalemate domino"—a reference to the game of dominoes popular among Cubans. Like *Now!*, this video showcases footage of police brutality, but this time performed by the Cuban police.

This song resulted from the specific censorship of artists and intellectuals that led to the creation of the Movimiento San Isidro—a political movement created in response to a law passed in 2018 that targeted artists and their freedom of expression. Decree 349 established harsh penalties against and criminalization of works not explicitly approved by the Ministry of Culture. Since the passing of this law, many artists have been arrested, including Maykel Osorbo—one of the artists featured in "Patria y Vida." In June 2022, he was sentenced to nine years for defamation of the country's institutions.

One of the founders of the Movimiento San Isidro, Luis Manuel Otero Alcántara, has become emblematic of Cuba's new fight for freedom. Like Che Guevara, his portrait has become a symbol. Performance art has grown in popularity in Cuba since the revolution, due to many artists' lack of resources—leaving them with the only medium they have available: their bodies. Otero Alcántara was arrested in Havana for simply draping the Cuban flag over his shoulders as part of a performance piece titled *Drapeau*. The piece draws attention to a 2019 law that regulates how to display national symbols. Recognizing his courage and dedication, *Time* magazine named him one of 2021's 100 Most Influential People. In 2022, he was sentenced to five years in prison.

Vida Profilactica

Another prisoner of conscience was Hamlet Lavastida, who was arrested while returning to Cuba from a residency at the Künstlerhaus Bethanien in Berlin in 2021. He was later released after fellow artist Tania Bruguera agreed to leave Cuba in exchange for the release of thirty-plus political prisoners.[7] Lavastida's 2014 work *Vida Profilactica* consists of X-Acto-knifed paper cutout drawings that examine and critique the iconography of the Cuban Revolution. The bold cutouts of people and type clearly reference the aesthetic of the OSPAAAL posters but strip away the seductive colors to draw attention to the revolution's violence and propagandistic gestures through the starkness of the white paper on the cardboard background. This stunning series is based on his research into the uncensored history of the revolution. Conducted while living in Cuba, Lavastida spoke with academics and others outside Cuba to collect information beyond what was sanctioned by the government. This project was conducted through spotty Internet access and underground content distribution systems such as El Paquete Semanal, a hard drive that delivers media (movies, TV shows, books) from all over the world weekly to subscribers as a way to circumvent issues with Internet access.[8] These systems create cracks in the facade of Cuban censorship that allow the Cuban people to access banned information and empower them to demand the truth.

In conclusion, Cuban graphics are as complex as they are visually appealing. They show us the power and enduring importance of bold and direct images and text—but require historical context to be fully appreciated. As designers attempt to broaden the design canon by exploring a more comprehensive range of cultures in design work, courses, and seminars, they must study and address the broader context in which these pieces came to be or risk further alienating the groups they wish to include.

ELAINE LOPEZ is a Cuban American designer, researcher, artist, and educator whose work explores the intersection of culture, identity, equity, and Risograph printing within the field of design. Elaine acquired her BFA from the University of Florida (2007) and her MFA from the Rhode Island School of Design (2019), both in graphic design.

KURDISH FRAGMENTS:
Mapping Pattern
as Language

Nuveen Barwari

imilar to a collage, this essay includes layers of information to reflect on various art practices in the context of the fragmented state of Kurdistan and its diaspora.

Borders and Spaces

During the time of Western colonialism, Western diplomats created national boundaries for much of the Southwest Asian / North African (SWANA) region. The Sykes-Picot Agreement of 1916 set up British and French mandates for the region with no regard for the ethnic communities of West Asia, the region now called the Middle East. Kurdistan was cut into four different pieces and occupied by Iraq, Syria, Iran, and Turkey. This occupation and division has led to genocide, ethnic cleansing, and state-sanctioned violence, which produced antistate resistance movements. It has also resulted in the diaspora of millions of Kurds who have been displaced, removed from their homeland, and transplanted into various host lands all over the world.

In "Decorative Art or Art Practice? The Conservation of Textiles in the Kurdish Autonomous Region of Iraq," Anne-Marie Deisser and Lolan Sipan discuss how Hamilton Road, the thoroughfare that runs through Iraqi Kurdistan from Erbil to the Iranian border, is a prime example of how economic factors may affect decorative arts. Built in the early 1930s, the road goes through the heart of the country. The route also enabled the British Army to bomb communities shortly after it was built, thwarting efforts by the Arab-Iraqi central government of the time to influence the British Army.

This action had a long-term and far-reaching impact on the settlements and nomadic tribes of this region's social and economic existence.[1] Following the completion of the Hamilton Road, the people in the region had to consider incorporating new aesthetic elements determined by Western sociocultural values and religious beliefs into their existing design lexicon to create or sustain healthy socioeconomic ties with the West. In new textile creations, these nomadic tribes varied the colors and motifs.[2] The shift in colors and designs may have been made for several reasons, including to appeal to new customers that the Hamilton Road brought in.

Erasure

Like its land and people, Kurdistan's decorative arts have a history of being erased, fractured, and branded by the region's colonizers. Kurdish rugs typically get categorized as Turkish, Iranian, Syrian, or Iraqi, depending on which occupied region of Kurdistan they originated in. This cycle of erasure goes beyond the walls of Western museums, institutions, and art history textbooks and seeps into the bazaars of southern Kurdistan. I had an interesting encounter with a proprietor of an antique shop in the city of Duhok during my most recent visit to southern Kurdistan in 2021. He would describe every rug as "Turkish" or "Iranian" but never as "Kurdish," even though they were unmistakably Kurdish rugs. When I repeatedly questioned him about whether the rugs were Kurdish or from the Turkish or Iranian regions that were under occupation, he finally responded, "Oh yes, sorry, I meant Kurdish. It's a habit when I sell rugs to Westerners, I tell them they are Iranian or Turkish because those are more popular."

The Making of Kurdish Rugs

Handwoven Kurdish rugs are made from a combination of natural and synthetic dyes, cotton, and wool. The Bijar district is listed as the third-biggest weaving center in Iranian Kurdistan in *Oriental Rugs—Smithsonian Illustrated Library of Antiques*. Bijar rugs, known as the "iron rugs of Persia," were traditionally made entirely of wool, but most current bijar rugs incorporate cotton warps and wefts.

Hand-woven rugs are made to be robust and long-lasting, though they were dismissed as difficult to maintain by colonists who would walk on them every day while wearing shoes. Westerners would eventually commercialize and mass-produce rugs that were more fit for their lifestyle. In doing so, they would also appropriate the symbols and designs of tribal and nomadic rugs for years to come, which led to a decrease in handmade rugs in the region. However, there is a vast contrast between the designs of handwoven rugs and those that are industrially manufactured. Patterns on commercially produced rugs are frequently generated using software to ensure perfect symmetry, while the imperfections of the handmade process are not looked down on in non-Western cultures.

Kurdish rug purchased from an antique shop in southern Kurdistan and described by the shop owner as Iranian.

The Art of Disguise

At certain points in history, it has been illegal to sing, educate, or speak in Kurdish. Out of fear of the authoritarian regimes controlling their territory, artists in Kurdistan have historically been required to conceal their ethnic identity in their work. Instead of using the name Kurdistan, poets and musicians frequently substituted the words *Gulistan* (meaning "land of the flowers") or *Gule* in their poetry and songs and employed floral metaphors and themes within Kurdish rugs and other art practices.[3]

I learned about the Kurdish songwriter-singer and composer Eyaz Yusef from family members, from his songs, and from people who personally knew him. In Yusef's song "Welate min," which translates to "My Country," he sings, "Welate min baxce gulaye," meaning "My country is a flower garden." Kurdistan is not a country. In fact, the Kurds are one of the largest nations without a state. Yusef calling his country a flower garden not only conjures the importance of nature and landscape in the Kurdish psyche but also draws on the imaginary.

This reminds me of the patterns on Kurdish textiles and how they emulate nature. Even though Kurds do not have a country, they are profoundly connected to their homeland and intimately tied to the land in the diasporic setting. Well-known protest chants such as "The Kurds have no friends but the mountains" reference not only political conflict but also the geographic struggle of being surrounded by oppressors while tied to a friendship with the mountains that have protected them for centuries.

Yusef has another song called "Gulek tine besi mine," which translates to "There's Only One Flower for Me." The meaning of the entire song has been debated and deconstructed by listeners for years— whether it refers to his lover or his stateless nation. Textiles, like language, can be cut, manipulated, and reassembled to disclose or conceal information. In Kurdistan's politicized environment, rug creation is a form of resistance. The different techniques act as a unique method of preserving, archiving, and documenting history, identity, and heritage. The carpets' patterns, colors, and symbols can hold political, romantic, and/or formal meaning.

Safety in Art

Women who experience consistent oppression often develop resistance strategies and an awareness of patriarchal politics due to their lived experience.[4] A lot of Kurdish women have engaged in crafting because of its relative safety. There is a link between the use of ready-made materials, the history of women in craft, and the Pattern and Decoration movement. David Ebony had a conversation with the curator and author Anna Katz for the Yale University Press blog about how the Pattern and Decoration movement has provided

> [an] effective countermeasure to the prevailing—
> and often stifling—dictates of Minimalism, which had
> ruled the art world with patriarchal authority since
> the mid-1960s. A serious socio-political agenda
> further underlies the glitzy surfaces of P&D works—

a visual manifesto centered on feminism, and an effort to overturn the traditional male-dominated view of art history as well as Western cultural chauvinism. At its best, P&D represents the first manifestation of cultural globalism.[5]

Many of the motifs in the Pattern and Decoration movement were inspired by non-Western decorative arts, which captivated the interest of artists for various reasons beyond aesthetics. For starters, many non-Western art traditions do not recognize a hierarchy or distinction between fine and decorative art. Women and people of color had long been dismissed as primitives and naïfs in Western philosophy and literature, incapable of major creative outputs; these labels were then used to disparage the decorative. Ebony noted:

> As the association between femininity and the decorative is a largely Western cultural construction, the vast field of non-Western art offered P&D artists (who were overwhelmingly white) a vantage point from which to reassess pejorative gender-based associations with decoration. As such, an immense range of motifs and art forms from cultures around the world informed P&D artists, who attempted to map and challenge multiple, intersecting hierarchies of exclusion.[6]

Repurposing Artifacts

Employing collage, painting, writing, textiles, and installation, I study the intricacies within conditions of assimilation and displacement and the contradictions within diasporic identities. My expansive studio practice involves gathering and repurposing artifacts from my community, such as worn Kurdish clothes, fabric, and used rugs, to investigate the multiplicity of materials, their inherited history, and cultural meanings, in a postcolonial context.

My textile-based paintings contain maps, symbols, and patterns that occasionally are revealed and concealed under layers of paint, concrete, and translucent textiles. My work is akin to the Kurdish dress, which holds layers of information, invisible labor, and a suppressed history. The floral patterns and symbols that I abstract from textiles often shift from being decorative to interrogating cultural symbols, redrawing borders, remapping, and reconnecting to ancestral land.

As with flowers, I am interested not only in the roots but also new acts of pollination and cross-pollination. Instead of focusing on what is often lost through translation, I vigorously sift through the different shapes and symbols that are found when one is living between clashing cultures, languages, and materials.

I noticed that my family had an extensive collection of old rugs, fabrics, and Kurdish dresses stored away in boxes and suitcases, and I thought others in my community of Nashville, Tennessee, might too. I put out a call on various social media platforms for traditional Kurdish dresses and rugs and have been collecting them ever since. I received bags of fabric, old Kurdish dresses, and rugs from the community. It was recognizable which fabric was from Kurdistan and which fabric was

Watering My House, 2022, rug cutout, concrete, thread, 8 x 10 in (20 x 25.5 cm).

Landscape, 2022, found fabric, denim, velvet, deconstructed Kurdish dress, thread, latex paint, fabric ink, 3 x 4 ft (1 x 1.2 m).

from JOANN or Walmart, although every single rug that I received from the Nashville Kurdish community happened to be machine-made in the USA. Making a home away from home results in a lot of settling for what is around you and what is available. Adapting, appropriating, resignifying, and improvising—the latter is an important part of my life and practice.[7]

Before I stretch the fabric, I cut and sew different scraps of fabric back together. Some of the scraps are left over from previous pieces. There is a sense of history, loss, and renewal in the way elements of the body are present and absent in my work.

It is hard not to associate the body with textiles; however, I find my work, like the term *gulistan*, to have multiple entry points. In this context we can connect the wrapping of fabric to the body or skin, but I believe that it would be appropriate to enter it in terms of painting and the pictorial plane, since they can be interpreted as landscapes too. What are these landscapes of? Who lives there? I think about this imagined space and the people who occupy it. Is it Gulistan? How does the wall become this imaginative space? Is it the wall inside a home or a bazaar? Whose body is it and where did they go? While I am dealing with deconstructing the word *gulistan*, I am also dealing with deconstructing the image of Gulistan, the image of the flower. Flower as patterns, patterns as maps, and maps as an attempt at locating "diaspora" or the space between a love song and a protest song.

The unstretched pieces are doing something that the textile-based paintings are not doing. They are larger in

Made for the Kitchen, 2021, latex paint, denim, velvet, oil pastel, bleach, 46 x 43 in (117 x 109 cm).

scale; however, they do not take up as much space as the stretched "textile-based paintings" do. They are fluid yet concrete. Rugs are architectural, and so are these unstretched pieces. They create and transform the space that they occupy. They respond to the environment that they are in. The unstretched pieces are nomadic in the sense that they can be rolled up and folded like rugs. Despite the fact that many people associate the rectangle with Western painting and make an effort to challenge that idea by breaking the rectangle and using shaped canvases, I find that by incorporating the

Cooking for the peshmergas, 2022, thread, Xerox paper, deconstructed Kurdish dress, 16 x 20 in (40.5 x 51 cm).

deconstruction of Kurdish dresses and commercially produced rugs into the world of Western painting, I am able to develop a new perspective on the rectangle and on Western painting because I associate it with rugs rather than traditional painting.

I have been making stuff with the women in my family. Flags? Rugs? Blankets? To cover bread. To clean the kitchen counter with. Funeral banners? Apartment-for-rent banners? While we make things we also talk about language, we talk about the politics of nation-states and borders, we talk about white walls in galleries and museums versus the walls that we decorate in our homes. We talk about Western feminism, we talk about redefining feminism—a feminism that includes our sisters, nieces, aunts, mothers, and grandmothers. We talk about small acts of protests. Patterns and decoration are indeed political.

In my most recent series, I've been deconstructing Kurdish dresses that I've gathered from the Nashville Kurdish community and using the portals that the heads usually pass through as the focus point. The fact that they resemble both head portraits and frames, as well as caverns, makes it difficult for me to think of a name for this series. On social media, there have been some breathtaking photos of Kurdistan landscapes shot from within caves that remind me of the textile-based paintings I've been making. The outlines of the caves frame the landscapes that are shown in these pictures. Although these pieces may be head portraits, I consider them in relation to caverns, landscapes, and even painting. When seen up close, caves may look enigmatic, stunning, and even frightening. Why do they seem frightful? Is it because we could be capturing someone's gaze back? Although most people find caverns uninviting from the outside, I think that, like mountains, caves may provide safety, companionship, and refuge.

NUVEEN BARWARI is a visual artist who employs collage to reflect on the fragmented state of diasporic living and membership in a stateless community. Barwari's expansive practice includes installations; performances; collecting and repurposing artifacts from her community, such as photos, rugs, fabrics, and Kurdish dresses; and an online shop that supplies apparel and art internationally.

COLLAGE and the BLACK AMERICAN AESTHETIC

An Interview with Adolphus Washington

If we look at the African diaspora in the Western Hemisphere, the group with probably the least African cultural retention will be Black Americans.... The eradication of African culture and the muting of it produced this kind of unique product. What I'm trying to do is produce work in that vein. I'm trying to produce work that is almost blues oriented—something that's part and parcel of Blackness.

—Adolphus Washington

Adolphus Washington is a Black contemporary collage artist whose work boldly confronts the conditions of the Black American lived experience. His design sensibilities are on full display in his work as he tackles complex issues through the use of dynamic compositions and a mix of visual textures. In my conversation with Adolphus he discussed his influences, intended audience, and the rooted messages behind his work.

Purpose

I'm still interrogating the Black aesthetic, and not the Black, African diasporic aesthetic, but the Black American aesthetic. In doing so, what I look at is art as a sort of propaganda tool and a teaching tool. In that way, I think my artistic lineage is rooted within the AfriCOBRA movement, along with the Black Arts Movement.

AfriCOBRA, the Chicago-based Black artist collective founded during the Civil Rights Movement, is known for creating vibrant, colorful work that illuminated the lives of Black people. Through the use of lively lettering, dynamic shapes, and visual rhythm, the group of artists developed an aesthetic style that bolstered the Black Arts Movement.[1]

In considering his work's purpose, his interrogation of materials, and how those materials are articulated into a piece, Adolphus remembered a quote by the cinematographer Arthur Jafa. Jafa states, "I have a very simple mantra and it's this: I want to make Black cinema with the power, beauty, and alienation of Black music. That's my big goal."[2] To that point, it became clear that it is the alienation of the Black American experience that Adolphus finds particularly consequential in the cultivation of its culture.

African Cultural Retention

Adolphus is careful with his word choice, deliberately using the term *Black* instead of *African* in most cases. "I use Black instead of African because it is important and more precise. When enslaved Africans were brought over on those slave ships, at a certain point, they ceased being Igbo, Mandinka, Wolof, or Yoruba.... They ceased being those groups, and they became Black." This distinction also points to the ways in which culture is developed and cultivated over time. "If we look at the African diaspora in the Western Hemisphere, the group with probably the least African cultural retentions will be Black Americans. And that's not an insult." Adolphus gave an example of the differences between the slave institutions in the United States compared with Brazil's and their residual impact on the descendants: "In Brazil you had slaves being brought in well after the dismantling of slavery in the United States. They were still coming in as an illegal trade." Adolphus explained that Brazil's longer-lasting influx of enslaved people created a large community able to sustain a greater amount of African culture: "You had these numbers, therefore creating like what we find with the folks in South Carolina and Georgia sea islands, the Gullah-Geechee people with a certain amount of retention that they managed to preserve due to the isolation." Referring to the descendants of enslaved Africans who were brought to the coastal areas of the Carolinas, Florida, and Georgia, the National Park Service writes, "Because their enslavement was on isolated coastal plantations, sea and barrier islands, they were able to retain many of their indigenous African traditions."[3]

> For those of us who may or may not be descendants of the Gullah-Geechee—the rest of us American negros were operating from a culture created in free fall, as Arthur Jafa puts it. Black American culture is one of assemblage through improvisation as a form of survival. The core principles within Black American culture are the oscillation between restriction and freedom; we express this through our music, art, and politics.

Because of this, Adolphus does not attempt to employ an Afrocentric aesthetic:

SXNDXY Service at Abyssinian, 2022, acrylic paint and collage, 16.5 x
23.5 in (42 x 60 cm). In 1808, several Ethiopian traders searching for
a place to worship found themselves at the First Baptist Church in New York
City only to then be segregated and ushered to the church's slave loft. This
discriminatory practice was met with resistance in the form of protests
by the Ethiopian traders and other Black members of the First Baptist
Church, who went on to form the Abyssinian Baptist Church in 1809. Since
then, the Abyssinian Baptist Church in Harlem has become an institution
rooted in advocacy, social justice, and political activism, particularly under
the Reverends Adam Clayton Powell Jr. and DeWitt Proctor.

Settler Colonial Revolt, 2022, acrylic paint and collage, 16.5 x 23.5 in (42 x 60 cm). The Revolutionary War for Independence, which witnessed thirteen colonies throw off the yoke of British colonization from the shores of North America by the American Continental Army, is a noble and romantic story. However, the quest for independence, led by General George Washington (center, above) wasn't a revolt to free all people from the instrument of imperial control but, rather, a settler colonial revolt of self-interest. Meanwhile, the enslaved, depicted bearing stars underneath General Washington, had their own ideas of freedom and independence and would later use Polaris (the North Star) as their guide to the free territories of northern American states.

Racially and culturally we're descendants of West and Central Africans, western Europeans, and Amerindians throughout the western hemisphere. Despite this commonality, the diffusion of slavery and oppression differed widely. There's a reason why the blues was developed in the United States and not calypso or capoeira, which explicitly demonstrate African cultural retentions. Within American chattel slavery, the process of eradicating and muting African cultural expression among the enslaved produced a unique hybrid culture accompanied by its own aesthetic....What I am trying to do is produce work in that vein; I'm trying to produce work that is a tone parallel to the aesthetic which produced the blues, jazz, and all forms of Black American cultural expression.

Artistic Influences

Regarding his influences, Adolphus explains that Jafa's ability to articulate the notion of a Black aesthetic provided a map for his own understanding. He goes on to say that he would be remiss not to mention Romare Bearden:

> I stand on his shoulders, that's just what it is. Growing up I wasn't aware of who Romare Bearden was, let alone his significance, but his work was always in the background. I even don't recall the first time I saw Bearden's work, but it was those shapes, hues, and overall style which stuck with me.

The Black American painter Jacob Lawrence is another source of inspiration. Adolphus mentioned the movement and sharp edges that defined Lawrence's style before going on to add, "There's all this intensity in terms of his work. There's a visual sound that encapsulates his work that is almost akin to...remember the show, *Good Times*? That painting with the people like this, and like that." (With his arms raised at an angle, Adolphus mimics the figures in Ernie Barnes's painting *The Sugar Shack*, which appeared in the closing credits of the 1970s TV show *Good Times*.)

There's a certain fluidity and yet intensity. It's almost like the way a sculptor achieves fluidity from materials such as marble, wood, or bronze. This effect is reminiscent of Jacob Lawrence's work, evidenced particularly through the *History of the American People* panels. It is this spirit which I try to achieve for the faces of my subjects.

Although he grew up in the South Bronx, Adolphus recalls a time when most of his childhood cartoon drawings had very Eurocentric features.

Yeah, I watched *The Jackson 5ive* and *Fat Albert* cartoons. I loved [Fat Albert] as a kid, but in most of our cartoons, the aesthetic was a Eurocentric phenotype and manner....So, it was easy for me to draw an aquiline nose and lips and features that were closely associated with so-called white people. Even cartoons which featured animals or non-humans, instinctively

Public Service Announcement for Colored (Not POC), 2021, acrylic paint and collage, 16 x 12 in (40.5 x 30.5 cm). The Black American political landscape has been fraught with Black political actors who have proved to be functionaries (of the dominant power) rather than leaders. A Black person who sets out to fight (for transformative politics) on behalf of Black Americans will be met with challenges from Black functionaries who aid and abet the arrested development of the Black community.

you knew they were either white or Black. Think about Panthero from the Thundercats and Jazz from the Transformers, who used Black American vernacular with the associated vocal inflection and tone. Any other cartoon character outside of these characteristics was basically White. You must shift yourself to looking at all the different phenotypes....of our Black American family and the diaspora....These are some of the influences.

Before moving on, Adolphus noted that he finds inspiration from musicians as well. After mentioning the saxophonist Kamasi Washington, he said that he is influenced by Nina Simone's artistic sensibility:

That's the thing. I'm trying to capture what sound looks like visually. If you're looking at this Black American aesthetic in terms of sound, there's also a visual aesthetic associated with it. What comes to mind automatically is graffiti being the visual expression of hip-hop or any number of Black American social dances like the Charleston or Lindy Hop, which correspond to jazz....This is what I'm trying to translate through my work.

Collage

Artists have employed the technique of collage for centuries, perhaps drawn to its mixed-media application and playful distortions of scale. While Georges Braque and Pablo Picasso are credited with bringing the practice to a mainstream audience and popularizing the use

Democrac(E)y, 2022, acrylic paint and collage, 16.5 x 23.5 in (42 x 60 cm). *Democrac(E)y* depicts the historical and systemic failure to include Black Americans in full US-style democracy. This is because the benefits of democracy for Black Americans have been mitigated by the social construct of race and its built-in consequences. The collage depicts Reverend Jones delivering the eulogy for democracy, which has died (again) when received by the very people who strengthened and expanded the boundaries through blood, sacrifice, material, and spiritual notions of freedom.

of abstracted geometric shapes within their approach, it was Black American artists like Bearden who infused the art form with jazz-inspired cultural stylings. Like jazz, the blues, and hip-hop, the soulful expressions of Black people often reflect their joy and their struggle. Adolphus Washington continues in the legacy of this work, as his collages provide the perfect visual device to express the layers and complexities that define the Black American experience.

Hard Truths

Adolphus's work isn't for the faint of heart or those unwilling to face reality. When I asked him if he is intentional in his messaging or if he creates work for open interpretation, he responded by saying, "There is absolutely a message in my work. In some instances, I can be considered a propagandist in that I'm looking to bring attention to the cliff that Black Americans are headed to—socially and economically." Though he is a self-proclaimed propagandist, Adolphus's work is factually based, even as it contains hard truths.

> I don't want to be an alarmist. But we are struggling and just surviving. Many are teetering on a knife's edge....There was a *Forbes* report that stated by 2053, Black American wealth would fall to zero.[4] If you look at our annual HUD (Housing and Urban Development) report, I think it's 40-something percent of American families who are homeless are Black."[5]

With Black Americans making up only 13.6 percent of the US population, the numbers are alarmingly disproportionate.[6]

There's also a very good study called *The Color of Wealth* published by economists from Duke University [and elsewhere].[7] This study focused on wealth stratification of various groups within the Black community in cities like Boston, Miami, and Los Angeles. They disaggregated the Black community into Afro-Latinos, Caribbean, African Americans, and Black American descendants of American slavery to focus on the median wealth of these groups respectively. What it revealed was each group's asset liquidity, and the results were startling. Black American families in Boston are worth like $8 liquid in comparison to Black Caribbean families' $12,000. In Miami it's $11 for Black American families compared to Cubans' $3,200. Lastly, in Los Angeles the total liquid assets for Black American households was $200; meanwhile, the African Black households' was $60,000. What I'm highlighting here is if you look at all economic indicators beyond this study… we're being plundered. I always tell people, just because you don't see tanks rolling through Harlem or any other so-called predominantly Black community, that doesn't mean that we're not under fire.

It's nearly impossible to ignore the topic of wealth when discussing the conditions of Black Americans and its impact on their cultural experiences. The *2019 Survey of Consumer Finances* reported that "the typical white family has eight times the wealth of the typical Black family and five times the wealth of the typical Hispanic family."[8] Adolphus says that the United States has

> profited off Black American wealth, which is bound up in our labor. In a Marxist way, we were by and large alienated from the means of production due to slavery and segregation—because *we* were the technology. As a result, this alienation has continued in many ways, which has mitigated our ability to accumulate wealth on a leveled playing field for generations.

Audience

Considering the messaging within his work, I asked Adolphus about his target audience. He quickly responded, "Black Americans. Everybody else can listen in….I'm not saying that every Black person likes my work. Essentially, as an artist I'm doing it for myself if I feel like there's something I need to say or that a conversation needs to be had." Regarding white and other audiences, he says that he loves the fact that other people can appreciate his work, but that he hopes it moves people to action.

> When I talk about statistical data in terms of where we are as a country and how we failed a significant demographic of our population….it's not meant

Priorities (Whitey on Mars PT 1), 2021, acrylic paint and collage, 16.5 x 23.5 in (42 x 60 cm). This piece is inspired by the late spoken-word poet Gil Scott-Heron's 1970 poem "Whitey on the Moon." The poem critiques the resources spent on the Apollo moon landings space program during a time when Black Americans were experiencing social and economic upheaval at home. Speed ahead to 2021, when we see history repeating itself: NASA successfully lands its Perseverance rover on Mars while Black renters experience the highest average rates of eviction in the country, during a global pandemic, with Black women disproportionately affected. I edited Scott-Heron's poem to fit today's Black American upheaval and historical benign neglect policy by utilizing my personal font (a nod to New York City graffiti) and centering the piece on the text as a message rather than the visual image.

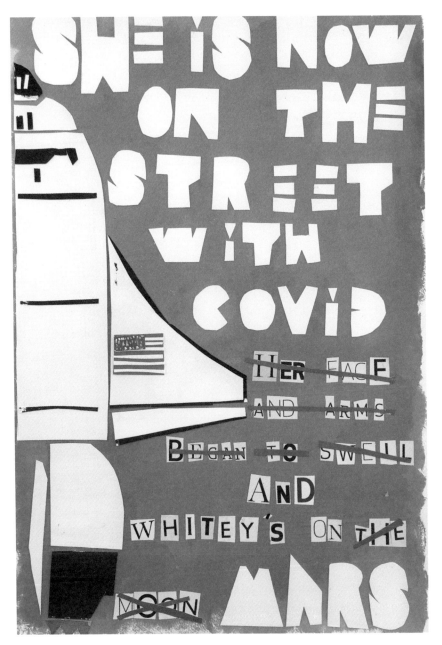

Priorities (Whitey on Mars PT 2), 2022, acrylic paint and collage,
16.5 x 23.5 in (42 x 60 cm).

to shame them. If it is shameful, I want you to be like, "Yo, where can I sign up? Who is the local representative on the ground?" Like, for example, there's the American descendants of slavery movement, or ADOS movement. Founded by Yvette Carnell and Antonio Moore, ADOS reinvigorated the reparations movement. It was these guys who, on a real grassroots level, held a mirror up to Black America in particular, saying, "Look, you're decaying, we have to address this." You know, I would love for my work to do the same thing.

Addressing a Black Political Crisis
"I have a piece titled *Priority* and it's inspired by Gil Scott-Heron's poem 'Whitey on the Moon.'" Adolphus recalls the pride and excitement of Americans in 2021 when the NASA Rover landed on Mars:

> During the Covid outbreak—when people were told to stay home while Black American women were most at risk for eviction, while Black male incarceration rate continued to be the highest among any ethnic group in the United States—I wanted to show fifty years of static social decay, from Scott-Heron's poem, published in 1970, to my collage bearing the same message in 2022. Currently, our Black political elite has forgone the reins of leadership and advocacy for a transformative Black agenda in favor of a functionary status where the priority is party over people.

He says that at the moment, we're in a Black political crisis, citing Harlem as an example, with the dismantling of political and housing protections.[9] Adolphus described the way in which companies have moved in and increased the cost of living. He called it a "decaying" of Black communities. "And so, it's those kinds of issues that I'm bringing attention to, and not just for the sake of being able to recite or regurgitate some facts, but as a call to action."

ADOLPHUS WASHINGTON is a Black American and native New Yorker who currently resides in London. As a lover of history and politics, his work seeks to capture the sojourn, culture, and sensibility of the Black American experience with a view to sensitizing his audience to the four-hundred-plus years of protracted struggle to be considered human, as well as American. Adolphus works primarily with collage, believing it to be the most democratic medium that best embodies the improvisatory nature of Black American culture.

THE TRUCK ART OF INDIA

Shantanu Suman

Indian Art Education under the British Rule

The British ruled India for almost two hundred years (1757 to 1947), making them the longest-staying colonial power in India, with more influence than any other European country. One of the numerous methods used by the British to reinforce their dominance was to change the country's education policies. In an article in *Studies in Art Education*, Ami Kantawala performs a deep historical analysis, referencing the work of multiple scholars to reframe Indian art education under British rule. Kantawala argues that even though the number of publications about the histories of art education has been growing, there continues to be a lack of discussion about the impact of colonialism on Indian art education: "In the limited studies that have been carried out, according to Dewan (2001), art schools in India have been represented as ineffective, alienated, and insignificant colonial institutions."[1]

Kantawala explains that during the mid-nineteenth century, four art schools were established in the British trade centers of India: Madras (1850), Calcutta (1854), Bombay (1856), and Lahore (1875), now in Pakistan. The schools' curricula were based on training in drawing and design that supported the colonial agenda—to increase revenue for the British Empire and to create work to fit the British taste:

> Goods would be produced that used Indian techniques taught by British officials and based on British aesthetic preferences. In other words, the rationale for establishing art and design schools was no

Hand-painted truck on the streets of Jodhpur, Rajasthan.

different from that of the Government School of Art and Design (GSAD) in London, namely for developing designs for manufacturing by promoting Indian handicrafts and to adapt their designs to suit British tastes.[2]

Kantawala also argues that schools in colonial societies promoted cultural imperialism. In other words, Indian students learned that European art was superior, more desirable, and positioned higher than traditional art taught in the Indian artisanal workshops.[3] Raja Ravi Verma, popularly regarded as one of the greatest Indian painters, is known for perfecting this European model and applying the regarded style to Indian calendar art.[4] The popularity of the magnificent Indian calendar arts launched a widespread distribution of cheap color pictures. Additionally, it led to the origin of other art forms such as matchbox art, hand-painted Bollywood billboards, and the truck art of India.

The Visual Landscape

While growing up during the 1980s and 1990s in an Indian small town, I witnessed a type of advertising that is vastly different from today. The streets were filled with vivid representations of popular themes, ranging from political messages and religious celebrations to commercial advertisements. Most of the work was hand-painted and crafted by local street artists rather than mass-produced using computer-aided design. It was common to find sign painters working under the scorching sun or hanging from wooden

Side panel showing messages about the business and the truck owner's personal and religious beliefs.

scaffolds, working from their sketches or magazine cutouts to paint large billboards and walls. Traveling from one part of India to another showed regional variation in style and technique.

Brightly painted wagons are a long-standing tradition in many countries around the world. Some examples are the Tap Tap buses of Haiti, the chicken buses of Guatemala, and the cycle-rickshaws of Bangladesh. In India, this tradition exists in nearly all forms of transport, as auto-rickshaws, cycle-rickshaws, taxis, and even ice-cream carts are decorated. Each vehicle owner ensures that his distinct character is reflected in the kind of vehicle he drives.

In particular, Indian trucks are transformed into a moving art form and personalized with motifs and symbols of nature, religion, politics, and even commercial products. Every surface becomes a canvas for communication. More than anything, Indian trucks are known for their sheer abundance and intricacy of ornamentation. Painted in vivid colors and adorned with rosewood carvings, the Indian trucks are often objects of extraordinary beauty and moving expressions of drivers' love for their vehicles. For a truck driver in India who earns his living by driving across states, decorating his truck can have many purposes. Some drivers do it to attract new customers and businesses, while others express personal thoughts and ideas. The decorations sometimes contain social, political, and religious commentary.

The *Horn Please* Project: Researching Indian Truck Art

Personal interviews of truck artists, with their profound knowledge of the trucking industry, became a powerful and effective way to gain firsthand information about the work and people related to Indian truck art. During a forty-five-day research trip to six Indian cities, including Mumbai, Raipur, New Delhi, Sirhind, Udaipur, and Jodhpur, I met with and interviewed truck painters, truck drivers, business owners, designers, advertising professionals, design educators, and art historians. Tracing the origin of the practice was difficult, since most of the people who started the profession of truck painting are now either deceased or too old to continue working. According to Seema Srivastava (art and design historian, New Delhi), truck art in India originated in the post–World War II period. In her

top: **Using spray paint, a truck painter applies base color to the truck's body in Sirhind, Punjab.** bottom: **Artist Raja Gharu painting a traditional village scene on the back panel of a truck in his workshop in Jodhpur, Rajasthan.**

interview, Srivastava mentioned, "During the war, most of the trucks were camouflaged in the army colors and were used to carry food and fuel for the army."[5]

Economic Influences

According to Balkaar Singh (owner of JP Roadlines, Mumbai), more prominent and well-known transport companies operated in earlier days. Owners invested in the aesthetics of a truck's exterior with good profit margins. However, over time, the road transport industry witnessed the introduction of more privately owned trucks, which increased competition and led to lower profit margins and less-decorated trucks.[6]

Identifying Roles

Within the trade, professionals whose work needs to be identified and distinguished are truck painters and writers/artists. A truck painter is responsible for applying base color to the truck body (using spray paint or brushes) and providing a smooth, shiny finish. A writer/artist, on the other hand, is responsible for pictorial art (designing the symbols and motifs) and writing the text onto the truck body. The selection of symbols, motifs, and text is made by either the owner, the driver, or occasionally the artist. Each theme painted onto the truck reflects the region the owner comes from, the religion he practices, his philosophies, and his likes. For example, Raja Gharu (truck artist, Jodhpur) confirms, "If a client (truck owner) wants me to paint Sridevi [a deceased Indian actress] on his truck, then I paint the face of Sridevi."[7]

Common text, symbols, and messages on a hand-painted truck back on the streets of Jodhpur, Rajasthan.

Messages and Meaning

In India, a truck is a canvas on which an artist expresses his thoughts and beliefs through an eclectic mix of popular phrases, figural images, and accessories. According to Mohammad Anwar (truck painter, Udaipur), the most common texts and symbols painted onto the trucks are the following:

Back: Horn Please, Ok Tata, number plate, 40 km speed limit, Stop, Signal, Use dipper at night
Front: Goods Carrier, All India permit
Side: Eagle, Mera Bharat mahaan (India is great) with Indian flags, cow and calf, lotus, etc.[8]

Though imagery and painting styles on Indian trucks vary from one part of the country to another, people can also find some common symbols on the trucks. According to Srivastava: "Taj Mahal is used so

Truck cabin decorated with vinyl and stickers in Sirhind, Punjab.

often. It's the pride of the world. The driver wants to equate and uplift the status of his vehicle to being the greatest of the world. Hyderabad has mostly Muslim truckers. So Muslim truckers will have 786 and the Kaaba and Karbala."[9] However, truck art goes beyond just being an instrument to make the truck aesthetically beautiful. Instead, on most occasions, it's a clever guise for displaying important information, superstitious and religious couplets, good luck charms and embellishments, messages of hope and victory, and the trucker's style. Prasanna Sankhé, an advertising professional, explains: "There are some daredevil persons who will write a couplet or a rhyme which defines or showcases their bravado, and there are some who are missing their home and missing their loved ones and they will write that message on the truck. So, it's exactly an extension of your personality."[10] Poor living and economic conditions and the dangerous nature of their jobs often leave truck drivers to find joy in the beauty of their ornate trucks. During years spent on the road away from home, drivers develop an overpowering affinity for their vehicle. One driver, Juhoor Ahmed, says, "When we decorate the truck, when we drive the truck…it should look like a beautiful bride."[11]

A Dying Art Form?

Contemporary economic challenges have put a strain on authentic handmade truck art. Increasing customer demand for faster truck production has resulted in the availability of factory-made decals and vinyl stickers, which many truckers do not shy away from using. Handmade truck art takes more human hours and is often an expensive luxury in times of wafer-thin margins. Introducing spray paint, decals, and stickers have made the job easier by replacing laborious work with faster and more easily applied options.

The promise of a better quality of life has made many truck artists discourage their children from entering their profession. Truck art has witnessed a significant shift in Indian society, where a son proudly takes on his father's occupation. However, truck artists who received a low level of formal education due to the poor economic conditions now earn enough to support their families, and they want their children to study more and find a job with more comfort and less human labor. The truck artist Mohammed Ashraf explains, "It'll be good if they study well and get good jobs. They should get jobs in air-conditioned offices, which is what I wish for. Rest is up to their wish and destiny."[12]

top: **Truck artist Mohammed Ashraf in Udaipur, Rajasthan.**
bottom: **Decals and vinyl stickers on a truck in Sirhind, Punjab.**

Wired magazine editorial spread designed and hand-painted by Shantanu Suman and Marisa Falcigno.

What's Next? Indian Art Today

My research and work on the *Horn Please* project led to some powerful and unconventional experiences. The success of this project changed the trajectory of my design practice and made me want to be an international designer with a vernacular flair. Over the last decade, I have been working with the theme of Indian vernacular design and the Devanagari script. It was very liberating once I stopped aping the West to find design solutions.

According to Merriam-Webster.com, *vernacular* means "a language or dialect native to a region or country rather than a literary, cultured, or foreign language." You will notice that the words *literary* and *cultured* are being used to differentiate the foreign language from a native language.[13] Upon further research, you can also find that the word *vernacular* is rooted in the Latin word *verna*, meaning an enslaved person born in the master's house.[14]

The Indian subcontinent is home to about fifteen hundred languages, of which twenty-two officially recognized languages are written using ten different scripts.[15] In 1835, during colonial rule, the British formulated an overall education policy for India using Thomas Babington Macaulay's report "Minute on Education." Macaulay, a British lord and colonial administrator, claimed that "a single shelf of a good European library was more valuable than the collected native literature of India and Arabia." And the first step in implementing this colonial education policy was to replace the traditional Indian languages by introducing English.[16]

Ever since the days of Macaulay, India has witnessed a cultural shift by implementing and supporting an education policy discriminatory toward the traditional local languages by rendering them "vernacular." These vernacular languages and typographic styles are essential in representing the local culture in a diverse country such as India. While English has become the necessary lingua franca throughout India, according to some native Hindi speakers, this is also an indication of the decline of Hindi literature, which was instrumental in India's resistance to colonialism. In an article for the *Bulletin of the Deccan College Research Institute*, Rahul Mhaiskar explains the term *Romanagari*: "Romanagari is a portmanteau morph of Roman and Devanagari. It is a vernacular word coined and used by bloggers and internet users. It refers to Hindi, Marathi, etc. text written or typed in Roman script as opposed to the standard Devanagari script. A possible reason for this is that Hindi-speaking computer and mobile users may lack tools necessary for typing in Hindi."[17]

Interior of a taxi in Mumbai. In 2014, Shantanu Suman, along with his copywriter, Shreedavy Babuji, collaborated with Taxi Fabric to design the interior of a taxi to promote a safe driving culture on the streets of Mumbai.

With Hinglish and Romanagari becoming popular, Hindi speakers are doing whatever it takes to keep the language alive in a world increasingly saturated with information conveyed through the written or spoken word. However, the spread of Hindi in Roman letters means that literate Indians are forgetting or not bothering to learn how to read the Devanagari script.

Coming from a previously colonized culture, I think some of us tend to develop two sides of our identity. One part gets trained to believe that the Western world is the North Star, and we try to mimic the culture of the West in our lifestyle, including our education, thinking, food, clothing, work, and behavior. This belief system can result from institutionalized education and work culture. But the other part of our training is based on our native culture, politics, economy, infrastructure, and overall reality of post-independence India.

For example, during my advertising career, one of the default design approaches was to use a Western design reference as an inspiration and put it into an Indian context. That led to work that seemed stuck in Western design models even though it was created by a non-Western designer. I had to work hard to unlearn that default approach; for designers like me, who come from non-Western cultures, embarking on a journey of exploring our culture through our practice becomes a challenging yet essential first step. Through some of my projects developed in recent years, I am hoping to bring more attention to the Devanagari script and the Indian vernacular style. For me, decolonizing design is not about being biased toward India or believing that my cultural heritage is somehow superior to others. Instead, it is about understanding that this is a process. Learning about my cultural past and present to create a better future is the key to culturally appropriate good design.

SHANTANU SUMAN is a graphic designer from India currently working as an associate professor of graphic design at Ball State University in Muncie, Indiana (USA). He has worked as a creative director, documentary filmmaker, small business owner, and educator. In 2013, Shantanu worked with a team to conduct his research and codirect *Horn Please*, a documentary film encapsulating various aspects of Indian truck art. You can view it at https://vimeo.com/shantanusuman/hornplease.

WOVEN IN ORAL HISTORY: AN INCOMPLETE TAXONOMY OF AMAZIGH SYMBOLS

Dina Benbrahim

Warnings

1. This is an incomplete story woven in oral histories and based on partially recorded stories as well as possible fabulations of collective memories. It seeks possibilities rather than just focusing on what is lacking.

2. This essay recognizes craft as design. The frame of Eurocentric graphic design history deemed craft unworthy of the design canon. However, in Indigenous spaces, understanding craft as design articulates new ways of knowing outside master narratives.

3. This reading has a prerequisite: a humble, open mind.

esign is a multidimensional, plural, vast, abundant, and ancient practice as old as this universe. Craft is not outside it, even if craft has had the negative implication of being "women's work." That is, if design is everywhere and in everything, from the planet to the universe, from artifacts to our humanity—leaving no space for anything outside design, separating craft from design becomes a limiting endeavor, acting against providing new spaces of knowing.[1]

Speaking of exclusion...many people have not heard of the goddess Tanit; read the stories of the queen Zaynab al-Nafzawiyya, the warrior Kahina, the ruler Sayyida Al-Hurra, and the leader Khnata Bint Bakkar; or discovered the priestesses Aristball, Geratmalquart, Omnastarté, Hotallat, and Kabdat, as these names were not a part of most history books in school. They were ancient women leaders across all social levels of the Amazigh, the Indigenous people of North Africa, yet they appear nowhere in Morocco's official history (and most likely not outside it, either).[2] Amazigh women have been leaders, deities, and agents of change in their communities since pre-Islamic times. Their legacy survives, despite the will of colonizers to erase it, in widely popular everyday-life objects such as rugs. These rugs appeared in the second millennium BCE with a unique knot and a geometric visual language with modernist qualities long before modernism.[3] In this context, Amazigh rugs are a powerful tool of collective memory, resistance, and innovation.

This research is a humble contribution to the urgent need to record, document, publish, and legitimize the overlooked narratives of Amazigh design through rugs. Historically, weaving stories have been curated and narrated through the lens of colonial, orientalist male ethnographers. This essay, however, attempts to study Amazigh symbology and metaphors from a North African, Moroccan, and feminist point of view.

The Pain of Weaving in Minds and Bodies

We cannot have a full understanding of the erasure of Amazigh symbology without exploring the complex system that contributes to this cultural loss. Socio-political, economic, and cultural dynamics have factored into the oppression of Amazigh weavers. To start with, Morocco has an extensive history of colonization, through the present day. Although the Greeks and later the Phoenicians were the first known populations to interact with the Amazigh culturally and economically, the Romans were the first to colonize the country throughout the third and fourth centuries CE.[4] The Arabs were the next population to colonize Morocco, with the establishment of the ruling Idrissid dynasty in 788.[5] More recently, Morocco was under the protectorate of France and Spain beginning in 1912 and ending in 1956.[6] Sebtah (Ceuta) and Melilla have remained Spanish territories since the fifteenth and sixteenth centuries.[7] The cultures of colonizers were imposed on the existing ones in various ways including through the local craft. In 1914, the French Protectorate initiated the Native Arts Service project to reinvent Moroccan craft through the lens of colonial values and aesthetics, which were nested in orientalist fantasies and "the modern taste" to appeal to European consumers.[8] These centuries of colonization reinforced cultural, political, and economic hierarchies; sped up the erasure of Amazigh design storytelling; and defined the status of Amazigh women as a non-elite underrepresented minority.[9]

Moreover, Amazigh women weavers continue to be exploited with intensive low-pay labor and confinement. In a conversation with Hamza Cherif D'Ouezzan, the current managing director at the Anou, an artisan-owned and artisan-managed e-commerce platform, he mentioned that 70 percent of women artisans come from a rural background and could not receive a formal academic education.[10] Formal primary-level schooling was introduced only in the 1990s in rural areas of Morocco, and the continuous lack of infrastructure still hinders accessible education.[11] As a result, rural women are dehumanized and constrained to the domestic space—where weaving is an acceptable occupation, often taught from mother to daughter and through marriage into a new tribe as an act of assimilation to the symbolic language and technique of the new community.[12] The rug market, being a heavily gendered space, systematically denies women weavers access. To sell their rugs, most women weavers have no choice but to use middlemen. In these markets, a middleman (called "dalal") grabs the rug from the weavers and walks a few feet away to meet another middleman (called "semsar") who will buy the rug and sell it again to the end customer. Of the end profits, 96 percent go to the middlemen, leaving only 4 percent to the weaver.[13] The humiliation from this inhumane process is often accepted because weaving is believed to fulfill a spiritual awakening by being a work of piety when executed to perfection.[14] This means that even if weavers experience physical pain from weaving and psychological pain from their exploitation by dealers, their true reward remains in another world.[15]

In 2018 Morocco had 425,150 artisans.[16] The export of crafted works outside Morocco accounts for 88 percent of all sales, with the total revenue of exported rugs being about $13 million in 2021.[17] Assuming that the number of artisans has not changed since 2017, each weaver would have received an average of only $1.20 from these sales, with the middleman model. Kenza Oulaghada, president of Association Tithrite in the Middle Atlas Mountains and a weaver and leader at the Anou, recalls a deep feeling of hogra ("heartfelt oppression" in Darija) when middlemen used to belittle her work by stepping on her rugs to devalue them.[18] Instead of counting solely on another world, she used her feeling of hogra to help rural women weavers by founding the first cooperative in her village and later the Association Tithrite.[19] With her activist drive, she created the possibility for change.

An alternative model to the dalal that existed in Morocco for decades is a fair-trade model that increases the weavers' profits from 4 percent to 20 percent.[20] This is still not enough to make a decent livelihood and even less adequate to create meaningful change in the sector.

Another aspect of exploitation happens in ministry-run centers and rug-making workshops where weavers learn the craft with no study of Amazigh heritage.[21] According to Hamza, middlemen within these centers receive government funding to hire apprentice weavers, but the funds are instead used to subsidize pricing, which automatically lowers the overall market value of rugs.[22] The Anou was founded with the goal to give power back to the weavers. The artisan business model allows the weaver to receive 100 percent of the profits. An additional 20 percent of the purchase price goes to the Anou as a premium incurred by the end customer.[23] That 20 percent is reinvested in the weavers' communities. The Anou currently works with over seven hundred artisans, and women weavers make up 70 percent of them.[24] It is a solid seed to fight against the severe exploitation of weavers. The model of the Anou successfully rejects patriarchal models that exploit weavers for a feminist one that empowers them.

Tikselt (Metaphors) of Weaving

Amazigh women preserved the Amazigh culture, heritage, and identity throughout centuries of colonization and patriarchy. Although political conditions influenced the meanings of Amazigh symbols across time, Amazigh symbology remains nested in mysticism and spirituality, as well as in the everyday life of Amazigh women and their experience of the land. Depending on the weaving technique, region, and color palette, Amazigh rugs fall into different categories. However, a common point the rugs have is the use of wool, which has been the preferred material for its symbolic link to fertility and the baraka ("divine blessing").[25] Among the most renowned types of rugs are the following:

BENI OUARAIN

Beni Ouarain is a region in the Middle Atlas Mountains that produces pile knot rugs. They have a minimalist aesthetic, often using a symmetrical layout and the natural color of the wool to represent good fortune and moral qualities.[26]

MARMOUCHA

The Marmoucha pile knot rugs are created in the Middle Atlas Mountains in the south of Morocco. They are directly inspired by the Beni Ouarain rugs—following a minimal geometric aesthetic, often in black and white—yet are shifting toward more asymmetrical compositions.[27]

top: **Beni Ouarain rug made by Malika Hdoudi, Fatima Yidri, Fatima Ahknini, and Fatima Adoudi from the Imelghas Women's Cooperative in Imelghas.** bottom: **Pile knot Marmoucha rug by Zarwali Tchfa from Cooperative Zarbiyat Marmoucha.**

left: **Taznakht rug made by Samira Oubrka from Association Timouzounin in Tadula Zanfi.** right: **Azilal rug made by Khdija Hamid, Wardiya Farh, Fatima Hamid, and Meriem Ait Bnali from Ighrem Timdokkals in the Azilal province.**

HANBEL

Unlike the pile knot, in which the weft is separated with rows of knots tied around the warp, weavers thread the weft back and forth through the warp continuously until the rug is complete to make a hanbel, also called a flatweave rug.[28] Hanbels come in a variety of vivid to muted colors.

AZILAL

Azilal is another region in the Atlas Mountains, south of Ouzoud Falls. Azilal rugs usually use the natural color of wool as a background, yet more-expressive exceptions are available. They are softer to the touch and integrate more vivid colors than the ones from Beni Ouarain or Marmoucha.[29] They are also visually more experimental and dynamic.

BOUCHEROUITE

Boucherouite is a word in Darija that describes the act of repurposing clothing and fabrics into rugs. This sustainable technique came out of necessity when families were low in supplies—especially during the cold winters of the Atlas Mountains.[30] Because they are dependent on existing fabrics, these rugs are all unique statement pieces, using bright color palettes and experimental compositions.

TAZNAKHT

Taznakht is in south Morocco. Their rugs are known for their vintage aesthetic using bright reds and earthy yellows, representing colors directly found in the regional landscape.[31]

Networks of Knowing

Archival and secondary research methodologies are limited by the collecting institutions and authors' interests. In design histories, our ways of knowing must expand to networks of knowing. In February 2022, I met on Zoom with Hamza, Rebecca Hoyes (a surface pattern designer), and representatives from eight cooperatives and organizations of Amazigh women weavers in Morocco working with the Anou: Association Tithrite in Ait Hamza, Cooperative Nahda in Souk el Hed, Cooperative Tiglmamin in Khenifra, Cooperative Zaouia in Sidi Yahya O Youssef, Coopcrative Asnli in Immouzzer Marmoucha, Association Afous Gafous in Ouarzazate, Cooperative Fadel Tighedouine in Tighedouine, Cooperative Talassine in Tounfit.

left: **Flatweave rug made by Fouzia Akallouf, Maimouna Bourchok, Fadila Aghray, and Maimouna Boujmmi from the Talsint Handicraft Association in Talsint.** right: **Boucherouite rug woven by Rabha Bawahi from Association Tadighoust in Qsar Mouy.**

Rebecca has been helping women weavers of the Anou foster their authentic design stories during online workshops. Rebecca believes that a story is the most important design tool, beyond shapes, layout, color, and technique. Indeed, a story transcends all rules of design when it is true to a specific heritage, as it bridges the personal and the political. In this session, weavers shared precious data on the meanings of Amazigh symbols woven in their rugs. They gathered this information after asking members of their communities to participate in their research. Kenza Oulaghada, from the Association Tithrite, started this research in 2003 out of curiosity about her own heritage. She mentioned collecting these stories from elder women in Ait Hamza who have now passed away, along with their knowledge. Rabha Houari, from the Cooperative Nahda, included the voices of her family, neighbors, members of the cooperative, and a highly respected woman named Fatima, commonly called "Mama"—as mother and authority. Likewise, Rachida Ousbigh from Cooperative Tiglmamin, Mariam Bertal and Aicha Bertal from Cooperative Asnli, and Halima Amami from Cooperative Zaouia asked their families and members of their communities to help with the research.

Though primary research did not allow for identifying the meaning behind every symbol, researchers came across common qualifiers and a variety of stories that are still important to record. Original meanings are unfortunately fragmented across communities, oral history, and very scarce written history. In doing this research, all weavers have realized how impactful it was to try to connect to their heritage. Rabha mentioned that before she conducted this research, she felt that she was walking in the dark, ignoring her stories in favor of technique. Naima Abekan, from Cooperative Fadel Tighedouine, discovered that some of their rugs are direct visual translations of prehistoric pictographs found on rocks two hours away from her village. Fatima added that the women she interacted with felt nicely surprised that someone would think about investigating their heritage. All weavers in the Zoom nodded, agreeing with Fatima.

Below is an invitation to explore our collective effort to create the first taxonomy of Amazigh symbols with their visual metaphors. These symbols are woven into rugs but can also exist in a variety of everyday objects. Some have been used in tattoos since at least the

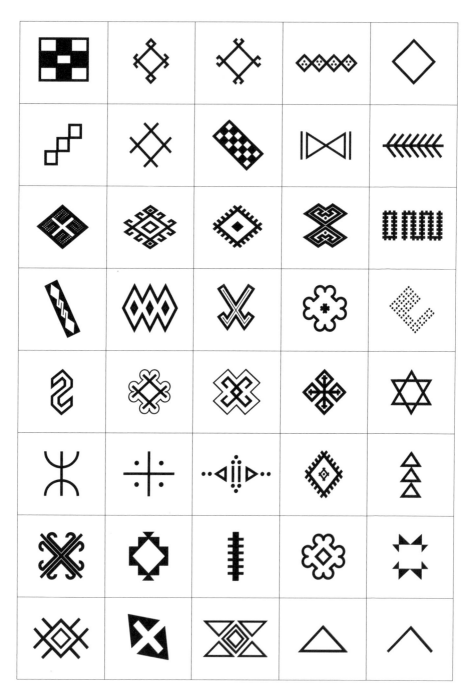

Incomplete taxonomy of eighty Amazigh symbols.

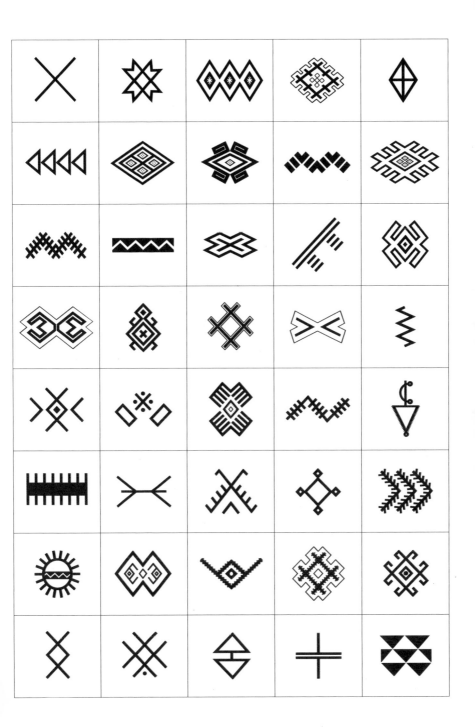

nineteenth century, although that has been rarely prac-
ticed since the 1970s due to an increasingly conservative
society.[32] This incomplete taxonomy of eighty symbols
and riddles is a seed that contributes to the Amazigh
feminist resistance through collecting, retelling, documenting, preserving, archiving, and publishing Amazigh
design stories from past and present memories that
will otherwise fade away in future memories. This table
summarizes the findings of women weavers through
primary visual research and my own secondary
visual research.

Conclusion

This essay is a deliberate yet modest effort to shift from
the world of ephemeral oral histories to ever-evolving
written histories. It aims to visualize the possibilities
of design histories when it does the hard work of illuminating overlooked narratives. To ignore histories is to
ignore our identities as human beings. The future of an
inclusive design canon first requires humility. Shifting
our framework of understanding history through a humble lens opens new ways of seeing and knowing where
knowledge production does not exclusively belong
to design heroes or scholars with a terminal degree.
It belongs to people like Kenza, Rabha, Mama, Rachida,
Halima, Aicha, Mariam, Naima, and all the women
weavers—their knowledge is equally as valid and
deserves to be recorded.

The impact of colonizers on the craft of Amazigh
weavers and their current deplorable conditions push
them to leave the craft industry altogether. The blatant

lack of interest in uncovering the pre-Islamic symbology found in the Amazigh visual language and even less in preserving their current stories also puts their heritage at great risk of being forgotten. Kenza joked with me, saying that she hoped I could be the next minister to represent the Amazigh weavers in Morocco. This subtlety highlighted that the Amazigh heritage might not survive without a sustained structural effort from an entire system that has been failing all weavers. Yet through the agency of Amazigh women using a platform like the Anou, they can at least start to reclaim their design stories and amplify their voices.

Acknowledgments

To the Amazigh weavers, I admire you and your revolutionary work. Thank you for trusting me with your precious knowledge. I am immensely grateful for all the help that Kenza Oulaghada provided in this essay. Thank you, Hamza and Rebecca, for your intellectual generosity and for introducing me to the women weavers of the Anou. Thank you to my research assistant, Kayla Spear, for helping me digitize the symbols.

DINA BENBRAHIM is a Moroccan multidisciplinary creative who uses an intersectional feminist lens to focus on illuminating the power in human beings to be transformative forces in society. She is an endowed assistant professor of graphic design at the University of Arkansas. Her research investigates design for visibility, civic action, and social justice for marginalized communities to collectively reimagine equitable futures.

AFRIKAN SOUL

An Interview with
Saki Mafundikwa

What about the pyramids? What about the Benin Bronzes? What about the terra-cotta heads of the Akan people of Ghana and Côte d'Ivoire? What about Adinkra symbols? What about the great city, the ancient city of Zimbabwe, the Great Zimbabwe, and so forth? But what about the magnificent cave paintings by the San people?

—*Saki Mafundikwa*

aki Mafundikwa is a Zimbabwean-born graphic designer, educator, and author. Published in 2004, his book *Afrikan Alphabets: The Story of Writing in Afrika* cemented his legacy as an international leader in design, as the book offered insight into the underresearched history of writing systems and symbols used throughout Africa. When I sat down with Saki, he talked to me about his origins in design, the challenges of running a design school in Zimbabwe, and what it truly means to live beyond the Bauhaus.

The Early Years

Though Saki developed an interest in art at an early age, graphic design was not on his radar. "When I came to America, I had never heard of the term *graphic design*, but I realized that's what I was doing back home growing up in what was then Rhodesia, the colonial name for Zimbabwe." In our conversation, Saki reminisced about how when he was a child, his father encouraged his artistic interest by buying him drawing books and crayons, honing a passion even before he was old enough to

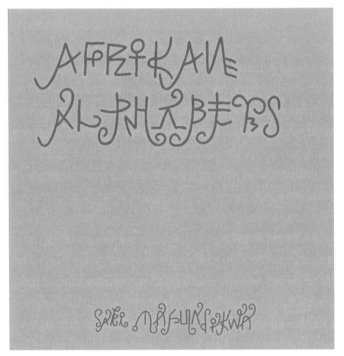

top: **Book cover design,** *Afrikan Alphabets*, **2004.**

bottom: **Type design for book title,** *Afrikan Alphabets*, **2004.**

go to school. While his early interest in art left no ambiguity about what path he would pursue in life, it was letterforms more than painting and drawing that intrigued Saki most. "I thought that all the letters, books, and everything were done by hand. I was like, these people are very good. I want to be like them." Little did Saki know, this very interest would later fuel his research in typography.

It was during his time studying at Indiana University in the United States when a Nigerian student living in Saki's dormitory first introduced him to graphic design. After seeing potential in Saki's flyer designs, the student took Saki to the graphic design department and introduced him to two professors who had gone to Yale, a connection that would later prove instrumental. When the professors asked to see Saki's portfolio, he recalled how little he knew about design. "I was like, my what? I didn't have a portfolio. So, they were intrigued. They said, 'Tell us about yourself, where you grew up, and what your parents did.'"

Saki explained to them that his father was a teacher, a carpenter, a builder, and a maker. He was good with his hands, especially skilled in carpentry. "Out of his sons, I was the chosen one to do the finishing, sanding down, and varnishing." He described how after he finished sanding something, his father would take a look at it from an angle and say, 'You've missed a spot.' The professors noted, "Oh, so he taught you how to see. What about your mother?"

After he described his mother to the professors as "just a housewife," Saki told me that they wanted to know more. They asked, "But what did she do?" After their push, he recalled to them that she was very good with her hands, that she crocheted doilies and table-cloths and was good at embroidery. In fact, his mother did everything needed to decorate the house. The professors exclaimed, "Oh, so you grew up in a house full of design." Based on that conversation, Saki was accepted into the design program. "They were like: you belong here. This is your department. And that's how I became a graphic designer." He was later encouraged by his professors to apply to Yale for graduate school and became the first African student accepted into the MFA program at Yale.

Afrikan Alphabets

At Yale, Saki was taught by esteemed faculty. His professors included the legendary Paul Rand, Bradbury Thompson, and Armin Hofmann. "My education was very Swiss. And I thought that in order to be a good designer, I have to be the best African Swiss designer I could be." Despite such a heavy Swiss influence, it was during his grad school admissions interview with Alvin Eisenman, the head of the department, that Saki was encouraged to look into African societies' writing systems. "I realized there and then during that interview that if I get in, that was going to be my thesis. And, of course, I did get in. And it became my thesis. And Alvin was ecstatic."

Though Saki wasn't convinced that his work was more than a synopsis, Eisenman encouraged him to publish his findings. "I wanted to do more research in Africa. I didn't even realize that I had found the thing that was going to bring me onto the world stage, in terms of design."

ZIVA

Even before the release of *Afrikan Alphabets*, Saki understood the greatness within African people, leading him to move back to Zimbabwe and open the Zimbabwe Institute of Vigital Arts in 1999 with a focus on design, new and multimedia.

> Multimedia brought in the aural too. You had to learn how to work with sound, not just with visuals, but also sound, motion, animation, etc., etc. I call it a brave new world—not a brand-new world, but a brave new world, where the student treads into uncharted territory. And because it's new, there are no rules. I always tell my students, don't use the archaic rules from yesteryear in creating today's work. They don't work anymore. In the past, we were taught "Don't be a jack of all trades and a master of none." But today, it's "Be a jack of all trades and a master of all of them." So, it's totally different. I'm happy to see this multidisciplinary approach to design, that even the term *graphic design* was too limiting. Visual communication can be anything. And it can be all things. Thank God.

Unfortunately, ZIVA has since closed. Saki explained that the Zimbabwean economy has been in free fall for most of the nation's forty years of

independence and that the country that used to be
Africa's breadbasket is now a basket case. A very sad
situation indeed.

The government that came in was more interested in
lining their pockets and looting the resources of the
country than developing the country. So the fact that
I ran a design school in a country like that, without
a single cent in funding—that's just a miracle. I'm beginning to accept that running that school for twenty
years under those conditions is an achievement in itself
and that I should be thankful. And I thank God, you
know. Because I always used to say, it's God's work
what we do as creatives. We are just like the pilots, you
know, guiding this plane. But actually, it's not our work.

Sankofa
I learned that all these so-called stars of design bow
at the altar of African design. We know there wouldn't
be any modernism if Picasso hadn't come across
African art. This is a fact. Africa is the source of it all.
And by extension, African people, African American
people, and Black people globally.

As we talked, Saki held up the book *Begin with the Past:
Building the National Museum of African American
History and Culture*, by Mabel O. Wilson. "This is what
I call Sankofa. Sankofa is our story. The people on the
continent, and the people in the diaspora. Our greatness
lies in our past." He spoke about the importance of looking back at the many achievements of Black people and

Album cover design, *Corruption* by Thomas Mapfumo and the Blacks Unlimited, 1989.

how important it is to recognize the work that has already been done by the ancestors. As an example, he brought up the work and legacy of W. E. B. Du Bois. "In this country, he's well known as a social engineer and an intellectual. He was the first Black PhD at Harvard. He wrote so many books [such as] *The Souls of Black Folk*, etc., etc. But what nobody knows is that he was a fierce designer." We both took a moment to reflect on this point, together referencing the incredible work in the 2018 book *W. E. B. Du Bois's Data Portraits: Visualizing Black America*.

Saki talked to me about the misconception that design is a European thing:

> What about the pyramids? What about the Benin Bronzes? What about the terra-cotta heads of the Akan people of Ghana and Côte d'Ivoire? What about Adinkra symbols? What about the great city, the ancient city of Zimbabwe, the Great Zimbabwe, and so forth? But what about the magnificent cave paintings by the San people who are erroneously called Bushmen? It's an insult. There's nothing like Bushmen. They are San. That's who they are. So what I'm saying is, it's not for a lack of material. Design has always been in Africa and Africans have been designers from antiquity.

As Saki uplifted ancestral work as examples of our rich design history, he also acknowledged how these stories have gotten lost and how history has been intentionally manipulated to favor the oppressors.

A lot of inventions that are ours are suppressed. We are not supposed to know about that. When they colonized and enslaved us, it was because it wasn't in their interests to glorify our creations and our inventions. How are you going to enslave or colonize somebody that you consider to be an equal? They had to demonize us. We were not human. The same way that slaves who came to America were not considered fully human. It's the same way that myself growing up in Zimbabwe in Africa, I was not human either. And so it was easy for them to steal our gold, our ivory, and use us as labor. I can't even start to talk about Native Americans, Indigenous people of this country—that was straight up genocide! So, we can't even talk about design before our students understand the importance of looking back at that history. In that history, comes greatness. That's where the design is....There is no way that we can talk of African and African American design without confronting the demons of our past. So yes, we have a common shared history. But from all that ugliness, great beauty can rise.

African Soul

Our conversation turned to education as Saki and I talked for a while about the importance of mentoring young designers. We were on the topic of HBCUs (Historically Black Colleges and Universities) when Saki asked me, "Do you know why I'd love to teach in the South? It's soul music. It's the music of my youth— I grew up on that music." He continued,

When I hear Aretha Franklin singing, "Never loved a man the way I love you"; when I hear that organ, what I felt when I was a kid listening to that, I still feel today. It's called soul music because you feel it in your soul. It's the same thing as jazz, blues, which is the classical music of America produced by Black people. That genius! We have it. Why is it when it comes to design, it's sold to us as a European thing? And if you can't design like them, your work ain't shit. That's the problem! We have to reverse that thinking. Why can't we see typography when we hear Aretha wailing? When we see Wilson Pickett rocking to "Land of 1000 Dances"…you know how we move. You know how Black people move? No one else can move like us. Who, under the sun? Why doesn't that translate to our design? You can give students a project. You give them Percy Sledge. "Come softly, darling…" You say, create this as a piece of design. Then you give them Mahalia Jackson doing a gospel thing. Tell them to design a poster based on what they're hearing. That is Black design. New Orleans, Professor Longhair, the Neville Brothers, Fats Domino…you know, genius.

Saki's voice breaks a bit. Becoming overwhelmed by emotion, he softly states, "That is going beyond the Bauhaus. If we can tap into that, we have gone beyond the Bauhaus." We both pause briefly for a breather. When he speaks again, he says to me, "I'm sorry. I get very emotional because this is very close to me. This is my life's work. And there's no need for it to stay here with me."

top: **Album cover design,** *Hondo* **by Thomas Mapfumo and the Blacks Unlimited, 1993.** bottom: **Album cover design,** *Kudada Nekuva Munhu Mutema* **by Chimurenga Renaissance, 2015.**

Beyond the Bauhaus

We discussed the design industry's adulation of Swiss design—a style movement defined by sans serif typefaces, grids, and abundant white space. Saki remarked that after his research of the African alphabets, his color sensibilities changed.

The Germans and the Swiss created white space because there is so much snow over there. They don't see color. We, people of the South, our lives, our skins...everything is the sun. I remember a designer saying to me, "Oh my, you're not afraid of color, are you?" That's something to be afraid of? Color? I mean, that statement stayed with me forever. But that's because that person had a Swiss design education, and to them too much color was bad. Why must there be white space? When I look outside my window in Zimbabwe, I don't see any white space. I see beautiful colors. And in any case, when I look at myself, I see all the colors. Because, as you know, Black is made up of all the colors. In my life, I am the personification of all the colors.

Speaking of grids, he said, "We don't have grids in Africa. Everything revolves around circles. That's our grid. That's our system." As we wrapped up our conversation, Saki left with these words: "We should not design to appease someone. We should design that which we feel from within. That story is very close to my heart because I have done that. I've gone beyond the Bauhaus successfully."

Book cover design, *From Adjoa to Zahara* by
Julia Stewart, 2007.

SAKI MAFUNDIKWA is a visual communicator,
design educator, author, filmmaker, and farmer. He
has dedicated his life to sharing Zimbabwean culture
through design, film, and education. Saki graduated with
an MFA in graphic design from Yale University in 1985.
He is a TED 2013 speaker and has led workshops and
lectures in universities throughout the world, helping
designers create a new visual language by understanding
their own culture.

RAZZLE DAZZLE: COLOR AND IDENTITY

An Interview with Zipeng Zhu

Color

I grew up in the tropical area of China in a city called Shenzhen. It's right next to Hong Kong. It's eight months of summer...two weeks of winter. It's warm, vibrant, sunny, [and] colorful. Our pride and joy is that we grow lychee for the rest of the world. Fruit, in general, in my city is unbelievable. So I grew up with lots of color. And flowers are everywhere. We're known as one of the garden cities of the world. We're very proud of that. So from that, moving to a city that is six months winter, with no sunlight, with daylight saving...it's difficult. And then, you know, New Yorkers love the black, the gray, and the navy.

I remember when I got here, I noticed during the winter times, everybody just became monochromatic because the city itself doesn't have a whole lot of color, unless it's at night. During the day, it's gray, brown, sandstone, pavement, and concrete. All of that doesn't seem very exciting to me. It doesn't really fit my persona.

For the longest time, the world [of] design was black and white and a hint of red. That was considered the gold standard of design. Sure, it had its time, but I'm not a person who's interested in repeating history. I'm interested in the future. I learned from what [has been] done, but you know, I want to challenge myself to create new forms, combinations, and possibilities.

Razzle Dazzle

I was watching the musical *Chicago*. In the musical, Richard Gere had a song called "Razzle Dazzle." It hit

New York Loves You signage at Ripley's Believe It or Not in Times Square, New York City.

me at first, and I wondered what it meant. You know, it's very vague, but then, somehow the word *dazzle* became like my middle name because it just captured everything. My name is Zipeng, which means "exuberant child" in Chinese. I want to live up to the name that my parents gave me and reflect that in my work. If it's a work that's made by Zipeng, I hope people can feel the energy, exuberance, color, boldness, and vibrancy from me. That's sort of the story of where I discovered color coming from—childhood all the way to college. All of these experiences sort of informed my love and passion for brightness, for energetic and fun graphics.

Life Influence

Being Chinese helps me in a few different ways. First of all, Chinese is a hieroglyphic language. So, all our characters are essentially graphics. They're icons. They're dingbats or Wingdings, for the designer in the house. I grew up seeing all the characters as images; when I got here, English became my first language in this country. It was very difficult because Chinese is not phonetically based. It's not about the syllables. It's about graphics. So I started to see letters as its own shape, versus the word. Also, I guess, I'm a little dyslexic. So when I see letters themselves, all I see is just shapes—slashes, circles, rectangles, all of these things combined. It's fascinating for me. As a graphic designer, I have this natural-born love for shapes. I would say, in that way, how I see Latin typography, it's very much influenced by my knowledge of Chinese. I usually try to illustrate with words as much as possible, just like a Chinese character would. So that's one side.

I would say the second side is actually my background as a biochemistry major. Math is a big, big part of my life. Almost every single work of mine is either built on a grid or an algorithm. So a lot of the things are mathematical equations. I recently just started to draw freehand, but prior to that, almost everything was built on a highly calculated grid. I am a person who runs on the number twelve. Everything to me is a twelve multiplier, so that's how I function. That's how I work, and that's how I live my life. It drives my friends nuts, but that's how my brain functions. Everything is on twelve. So yeah, I will say those two are the number one influences in my work.

Now, what's interesting is I actually manage to work on a lot of bilingual projects because of my background. I often get pulled in as a Mandarin or Cantonese consultant for brands who want to expand

Mural at the Global Visual Art & Design Exhibition Shanghai, Liu Haisu Art Museum.

their reach. I get asked for that somewhat often. And it's been really interesting. [For example], I get to help brand agencies craft Chinese word marks. It is extremely exciting merging a brand language to a completely different linguistic system.

Design "Rules"

In the past three years, social media started to challenge the aesthetic. On Instagram, if you go to explore what you find interesting, it's usually not the people who follow the rules. One of the things I [learned] at school was, "do not stretch your type." Everybody's stretching their type right now. What I find hilarious is, at school, sometimes you feel like there are these No! No! No! No's! And who decides that? What makes them the voice of God? Instead of that, I prefer to understand the supply and demand. What can you provide to the industry, and to the world, that's not there? I'm excited to look forward to the future, instead of the past. There are legends and masters already out there. Massimo Vignelli and Josef Müller-Brockmann nailed Swiss design. Let's do something else.

ZIPENG ZHU is a Chinese-born art director, designer, illustrator, and animator in New York City who wants to make every day a razzle-dazzle musical. Zipeng has worked at Pentagram and Sagmeister & Walsh and has had his work recognized by *PRINT* magazine and One Show.

top: **American Eagle Outfitters, Times Square, New York City.**
bottom: **#StopAsianHate Public Service Announcement for Times Square, New York City.**

NEW LESSONS FROM THE BAUHAUS

An Interview with Ellen Lupton

Kaleena Sales: As design educators seek ways to diversify their teaching materials and become less reliant on the traditional design canon, how can movements like the Bauhaus remain relevant?

Ellen Lupton: The Bauhaus (1919–33) was a vibrant and divisive place—like schools and design programs today. The Bauhaus was not just a school—it was a myth, an idea. The Bauhaus is a collection of artifacts, stories, and beliefs that have influenced design practice for over a hundred years. Even in its own time, insiders and outsiders sought to control the Bauhaus narrative.

Many women and immigrants attended the Bauhaus, where they struggled against stereotypes and bias. László Moholy-Nagy and Marcel Breuer (two of the school's most influential members) were Hungarian immigrants. Americans tend to group all Europeans together, but at the time, students from countries outside Germany were often considered Other. Jewish students also stood out. That said, as members of the Hungarian avant-garde, Breuer and other immigrants contributed inspiring alternative perspectives to the school. Moholy-Nagy, who joined the school as a lead instructor, brought Constructivism and the New Typography to the Bauhaus. Constructivism flowed directly from Cubism, a movement fueled by African aesthetics. Thus, there is no Bauhaus design without African art. Moholy-Nagy collaborated with Lucia Moholy; her role was underplayed by Moholy-Nagy and other men dominating the school. There is no Bauhaus design without the women who worked, taught, and studied there.

New scholarship explores the role of women, queer aesthetics, mysticism, and the experience of immigrants and refugees in the Bauhaus orbit. Educators today can tell much richer stories about the Bauhaus than what I learned in school forty years ago.

KS: How can we teach typography in a way that feels liberating and inclusive?

EL: Typography is for everyone. It's not a secret art. We use typography constantly, whether texting, making a brand logo, or posting to social media. Some design-world discussions of typography are pointlessly exclusionary. Consider the conversation around the terms *font* and *typeface*. In everyday life, both words refer to the appearance and style of letterforms. Yet some experts chastise people for using *font* to describe anything other than software or technology.

Pushing one way of doing things is also exclusionary. For example, in my own practice, I have long embraced grids as the single most important structure for organizing content. Yet before the rise of the Swiss grid, commercial art manuals taught design workers how to create dynamic, varied mixtures of type and image. What other methods have been erased or overlooked? What new methods can we create? Embracing just one method makes it hard to see or imagine alternatives.

KS: Can the canon be elasticized without bursting? (If we continue to expand the definition of design and include additional methods and ideologies, who or what becomes the voice of authority?)

EL: Design history isn't a zero-sum game. Adding new narratives doesn't require deleting all the old ones. Historians and educators can unpack and explode the narrative of modernism. How did artists and activists seek to change the status quo? What practices got pushed to the margins from definitions of "good design"? Who was working in the background? Who was excluded? How have marginalized communities used design to preserve and expand their own heritage?

Instead of seeking one voice of authority, let's develop an open set of tools, approaches, and origin stories. Many design history instructors are replacing linear chronologies with thematic groupings. Topics such as ornament, craft, industrialization, literacy, and publishing offer opportunities to talk about colonization, women's work, labor practices, and the global trade in styles. The canon IS elastic. Students can study principles such as geometry, symmetry, grids, and modularity by exploring examples and ideas from around the world.

The canon is transmitted not just in history courses, where students sit in dark halls watching PowerPoint shows. The canon is built every time instructors share precedents from history or from contemporary practice. Educators can find exemplary work created by people of color, people from different parts of the world, and people with different genders and abilities. Sharing this work requires conscious effort. Luckily, today's community of scholars, journalists, and designers is assembling archives, books, online courses, and other resources.

KS: As we begin to challenge metaphorical monuments in design history, some educators (and designers) are left feeling unsure of what to do in the absence of a dominant and authoritative style voice (i.e., Swiss design). How can we maintain a "discipline" of design without reliance on a set of "norms"?

EL: Society runs on norms. Perhaps that's what a society is: a set of norms governing collective beliefs and behaviors. Some norms are potentially valuable to everyone—traffic laws, say, or basic values of respect and kindness. Some norms are oppressive, including restrictive categories of race, gender, class, and ability. Social norms are constantly being expanded or diminished, including civil rights and human rights.

The norms of graphic design have developed over hundreds of years. Design norms include concepts of legibility, readability, hierarchy, consistency, color matching, web protocols, typeface licensing, intellectual property, accessibility, and so much more. These norms generally benefit readers, writers, and creators. They also benefit businesses and institutions—sometimes at the expense of workers and the planet. Some works of design push against norms and begin to craft new ones. The typographic grid is a useful and beneficial norm—as long as it's not promoted as the only way of working.

Insisting that designers only produce protest posters, illegible typography, speculative installations, or personal experiments would be elitist in its own way. Many people enter the design field intending to create work that is legible, accessible, and economically viable. Such work relies on established norms of practice. I do think designers can work creatively within design standards and contribute to the social good. Designers can also discuss, critique, and mend the various ways that design favors systems of power. Designers should always consider how their work supports their own values.

KS: What excites you most about the future of design?

EL: Students are demanding more inclusive histories. I'm excited by all the students, scholars, critics, historians, and designers who are questioning fundamental assumptions, exposing bias, listening to suppressed voices, and uncovering the capitalist, colonialist, and racist drivers of industrial culture. People of privilege were taught that modern design aimed to improve the lives of everyone. Today, we know that isn't true, despite the good intentions of many brilliant designers—at the Bauhaus and elsewhere.

Design can illuminate and liberate. Design is also a job and a profession. As more diverse voices join the profession, the visual language will expand. The profession will change, and so will the ways that designers teach and learn.

ELLEN LUPTON is a writer, curator, educator, and designer. She is Betty Cooke and William O. Steinmetz Design Chair at Maryland Institute College of Art and curator emerita at Cooper Hewitt, Smithsonian Design Museum. Ellen is the author of numerous design books, including *Thinking with Type* and *Extra Bold: A Feminist, Inclusive, Anti-Racist, Non-Binary Field Guide for Graphic Designers.*

VOCAL TYPE

An Interview with Tré Seals

Design and Meaning

I had no understanding of type design, but I started drawing my first typeface during my senior year of high school. It was this series of sans serif letters wrapped in ribbons, essentially. It looked like they were unraveling around these letters. I released it as a vector font in 2013 and called it Unveil, like five different styles. It was essentially just Futura wrapped in ribbons because I still didn't know how to design type professionally. On a personal level, the design was inspired by my experience as a two-time brain tumor survivor. In the end, it looked like my bandages were coming off.

History and Culture-Specific Work

I've always been a huge fan of history. I live on a farm that was built by my great-great-great-grandparents back in 1911. They owned a large portion of the town I live in. They would only sell land and loan money to Black members of the community, because the banks wouldn't loan them money. So, they would sell property to other Black families to basically have their own legacy. I still live on that farm today with my parents. My parents live in the house that my great-great-great-grandfather built. My studio that I'm in right now used to be the stable, and my house used to be the chicken coop. I've been surrounded by history my entire life, pretty much, so I've always loved history. Just from a cultural perspective, I experienced racism for the first time way back in the third grade. I've been aware of it ever since. That was when I was in Catholic school. A year later I went to an international day school, where there was only one white person and everyone else was either Black or Hispanic. We were taught Black and Brown history and learned about all these amazing things we invented. That just made me want to explore Black and Brown history even more after that. So, when it came time for me to start Vocal Type, I had already known about the "I AM a Man" signs since fourth grade. That's why Martin was the first [typeface] I made.

Appropriation

From my perspective, I feel like appropriation is stereotyping of culture. I feel like appropriation of the Black community is only using red, green and black and yellow…or like making a font inspired by the Arabic handwriting in English. I feel like that's appropriation because you're just basing your work off a stereotype. When you show research that really honors that culture that you're trying to represent, I feel like that is not appropriation. I started Vocal as a way to diversify design. When culturally specific typefaces are used, it adds to the design diversity because it takes messages of various cultures and puts them in places where those cultures would never normally be seen or heard. I thought it was so amazing when this company in London actually used Eva, which was inspired by the women's suffrage movement in Argentina. This company used it for a white-owned third-generation men's fashion brand in all their advertising. That's cool because you probably wouldn't otherwise see any of that in those spaces.

MARTIN

We Shall Overcome! Deep in my HEART, I do believe that We Shall Overcome!

Typeface: VTC Martin.

HOW MANY YEARS HAS IT TAKEN PEOPLE TO REALIZE THAT WE ARE ALL BROTHERS AND SISTERS AND HUMAN BEINGS IN THE HUMAN RACE?

VTC RUBY
ABCDEFGHIJKLMN
OPQRSTUVWXYZ

Typeface specimens: top: **VTC Marsha**. bottom: **VTC Ruby.**

Empathy

When I graduated from college, I decided to take a full-time position at a staffing agency in Washington, DC. Over the course of two years, I worked for nine different companies for a minimum of a month. And at all those companies, I was either the only one or one of two people of color in the entire office. I remember there was this one company where we had weekly staff meetings where there were like ten offices...and I was still the only Black person in the room. When I think of empathy, I think about cultural sensitivity. I started Vocal while I was working at this company. So when I thought about diversity and empathy, all those things were going through my mind at that time.

Black Cultural Influence

I've recently been learning about the expansive influence of Black culture. I've been researching other movements outside Black and Brown culture. Right now, I'm doing a font inspired by the protests in Tiananmen Square in China, and there was a protest sign in English that actually said, "We Shall Overcome." There was actually an "I AM a Man" sign that was held up during the Arab Spring. I feel like we've set the tone for what protests look like. From that perspective, I feel like you should infuse your culture in everything you do.

TRÉ SEALS is founder of Vocal Type, a type foundry for creatives of color who feel they don't have a say in their industry and want to tell the stories of the people we serve, not the false history of the industry we work in.

DECOLONIZING GRAPHIC DESIGN: A MUST

Cheryl D. Holmes Miller

I n 2022, I had the honor of being the honorary doctorate awardee and keynote commencement speaker for both Maryland Institute College of Art (MICA) in Baltimore and Rhode Island School of Design (RISD) in Providence. In each scenario, I was parked on the front row of faculty seating. I sat directly next to the diploma table, at an angle to the microphone and podium. For each college, respectively, the president and provost awarded the degrees by category and candidate to the graduates.

I couldn't believe my eyes. At MICA, I leaned over to my right. I whispered to the other awardee (she was Asian), "There is quite a large pan-Asian community graduating today!"

"They are the international student population," she informed me. When I got to RISD, I didn't need her by my side to explain the dynamic pan-Asian community walking across the commencement stage. The visual representation was expansive.

Today, there are fewer and fewer white students in art school. Although it varies by region, the white student population has dwindled everywhere in the United States. I know that might be shocking. I saw it coming. I knew the change had already come. The shift had shifted.

I knew fear would overtake "the Academy." The white dominant culture has been in disbelief, suddenly forced to address decreasing enrollment numbers. Keeping sacred tenured professorships cemented in today's art colleges and universities is challenging. The art school student population is now varied and extremely mixed by culture, ethnicity, race, creed, color, and gender. I gazed at the Northeast Corridor's 2022 commencement graduates lined up marching. I didn't need data research to tell me the graphic design historical canon is old news, attempting to broadcast to a more diverse and international art and design scholar. I knew the collision—not an intersection, but a collision—of the Eurocentric white male–centered canon of graphic design and the changing demographic of today's art college and university studio classrooms would become intolerable. With this type of paradigm shift comes a list of demands! The twenty-first-century art and design student body is demanding more than Euro white male professors with sterile pedagogies and unspoken, unquestionable, undeniable biases. Graphic design history books must be rewritten. New, revisionist editions and new, decolonized editions must include more stories.

Instagram has been the "call-out," "take-down" bulletin board for demanding change. "Decolonize," "De-Center Whiteness," "White Default," "Dismantle White Supremacy," "Eradicate Systemic Racism," "Anti-Racism Design Justice" posts flood Instagram daily from disgruntled students demanding more than Euro white male design pedagogy. "Ol' school" white male design professors have become just that: old. The students are winning both the battles and the war for a more diverse, inclusionary, and equitable art and design academic education; even the white ally design scholars are demanding change.

For decades, no one was paying attention, or they didn't believe, or they were in denial of the forecast. Headlines alone tell the future, beginning with the Pew Research Center: "Explaining Why Minority Births Now Outnumber White Births" (Pew Research Center, 2012), "For U.S. Children, Minorities Will Be the Majority by 2020, Census Says" (NPR's Bill Chappell, 2015), "The US White Majority Will Soon Disappear Forever" (the *Chicago Reporter*'s Dudley Poston and Rogelio Sáenz, 2019).[1] The forecasting headlines didn't have to tell me twice; my own children's Generation Z and my nephew and niece's Generation Alpha, as well as their friends, are already here! Year after year, the forecast has been predicting the paradigm shift.

The future has arrived. *People* magazine finally announced that tomorrow has arrived today: "2020 Census Data Shows White Population in the U.S. Declined for First Time on Record"; "shrinking" (AP and Yahoo News); "shrank" (Reuters); "less and less white" (*New York* magazine).[2] These 2021 reports broadcasted the major shift in how the US Census shows us just who we are: a melted pot.

More important, "What do we do?" is the pertinent question. The University of Texas Austin School of Design and Creative Technologies heard their own student and alumni clarion call for a new pedagogy and for a more diverse as well as inclusive graphic design studio classroom. In the academic year 2021–22, their website reported that of approximately 187 total design undergraduates, 66 were white. An admissions representative helped me to interpret that approximately 121 students could be considered BIPOC (65 percent), using the broadest possible description of BIPOC. (*BIPOC*, meaning "Black, Indigenous, (and) people of color," is a familiar term in academe, used to categorize the genre of everyone who is *not* white. The term sheds insight into understanding the historical oppression of people of many colors found in the collective histories of North American and US history and beyond.)

Identifying a pool of diverse professors and cluster hires as well as unionizing faculty have been starting initiatives in answering the call for a new pedagogy and safeguarding this new, diverse community. In the spring of 2021, the university offered me an opportunity to develop my course "Decolonizing Graphic Design: A Black Perspective." Roger Williams University in Providence, Rhode Island; Howard University in Washington, DC; and Art Center in Pasadena, California, have extended the same offer for me to teach my course. At the close of the semester in 2021, UT offered me the revered E. W. Doty Professorship in Fine Arts to support my continued research and writing of new histories.

Surveying the top design programs around the country, I find that Yale School of Art in New Haven, Connecticut, is engaged in a bold new strategy. Appointed in 2021, Kymberly Pinder is the school's first Black dean. Dean Pinder ('95 PhD) is an internationally recognized scholar of race, representation, and murals. This is an anomaly, and I just had to ask her what Yale would have her accomplish. Dean Pinder replied to me in a candid conversation, "I was hired to create an inclusive and holistic vision for Yale School of Art's future. I am charged to review Yale's 152-year-old structures and cultures to establish the twenty-first century vision for the next 150 years."[3]

Dean Pinder has begun to implement visionary new strategies to foster a new Yale School of Art. In June 2022, Yale announced a new director of graduate studies in graphic design, Nontsikelelo Mutiti. A Zimbabwean-born visual artist and designer, Mutiti is the third director of the revered graphic design department, following Professor Sheila Levrant de Bretteville's thirty-two-year tenure.

Furthermore, in July 2022, the Association of Independent Colleges of Art and Design (AICAD) announced that Yale School of Art was approved for membership by the Board of Trustees. It is the first new member since the association's bylaws were updated and enforced in 2019, with its adoption of the "AICAD Statement of Principles on Diversity, Equity, and Inclusion." The new bylaws state a commitment to a broader community and acknowledge "that structural, systemic, historical, and intersecting forms of oppression require our ongoing attention, action, innovation, and leadership for positive change," that "thinking and making requires the full embrace of diversity, equity and inclusion," and that our duty is to provide "learning environments and communities within which all can succeed."[4]

After a series of bomb threats to historically Black colleges and universities (HBCUs), AICAD president and executive director Deborah Obalil and board chair

Elissa Tenny addressed the AICAD community in February 2022 by issuing a letter declaring that AICAD stands with HBCU members against violence and intimidation.[5]

In a recent article in the AIGA Design Educators Community newsletter, Kristina Lamour Sansone, professor of design at Lesley University College of Art and Design, reports her new pedological data for her senior capstone and portfolio development class in the academic year 2021. We collaborated in teaching this senior design class, in which fifteen out of the eighteen students (83 percent) were BIPOC. The class had three white students. By asking me to co-teach, she wanted to explore how a senior design course could provide opportunities to dismantle structures, provide open space, and build new learning architecture given the increasing BIPOC student demographic in predominantly white ACAID schools. Professor Sansone, ahead of the curve, realized the demand for new approaches. She was correct! The net take: 62 percent of her senior class secured their first employment opportunity or entered graduate programs within three months of graduating in May–June 2021; during the first year of a global pandemic, her class had both survived and thrived.

In "Black Designers: Forward in Action," the last of my *PRINT* magazine trilogy of themed articles, "Black Designers Missing in Action," I included new data from RISD. During the Civil Rights era, after the assassination of Martin Luther King Jr. in 1968, RISD was among the first cadre of academic leaders of the midcentury era to begin diversifying their student population. Thus, I found myself at RISD in 1970 as a freshman, having been admitted through their Minority Recruitment Program. Since then, I have been keeping up with their diversity data.

Recently, I discovered the history of the student-led RISD and Race Forum, organized in 2020 to confront racism experienced in the RISD community and the lack of support the school provides BIPOC students. Voice after voice spoke their truths. The RISD community was demanding that the institution make immediate changes in a response to its outcry.

"'Out of My Element': The Experiences of Black Art Students in Critique" was researched and written by then–RISD psychologist Dr. Erin N. S. Unkefer and colleagues, and published in the *Journal of Diversity in Higher Education*.[6] The 2021 report casts a halogen light on educational inequalities and the need for a culturally expansive and more inclusive pedagogy. It is a scathing report; Unkefer reports on RISD's Eurocentric teaching practices and is not bashful in calling out other renowned ACAID schools, as well.

I dug deeply into RISD's current situation for my *PRINT* article. I found RISD's Matthew Shenoda, the former and first-ever vice president of Social Equity and Inclusion at the helm. He reported that out of 2,500 students in 2019, 94 were Black. The total BIPOC community of LatinX, mixed-race, Black, Native American, and unspecified backgrounds represents 494 students, which doesn't include the Asian population of 397 students. According to RISD data, the total BIPOC community at the school in 2019 encompasses 19 percent of the student population, of which 3.8 percent is Black.

These are not great statistics; they offer great challenges. The RISD students presented a long list of demands to the administration, which was summed up by Jada Akatao at the RISD and Race Forum: "We demand that RISD reckons with its role as a beneficiary of white supremacy. As a wealthy cultural institution within the United States, RISD cannot exist without exploiting the labor and lives of Black and Brown people in this country and around the world. We want reparations and an intense restructuring of its intra-institution and inter-institution racial dynamics."[7] The RISD student body has spoken; the student-led RISD Anti-Racism Coalition (risdARC) and a group of BIPOC faculty along with the administration are committing to a new set of actions to inspire a better RISD. "As the leader of RISD, I take responsibility for having allowed a culture to continue to exist that does not fully live up to our values," RISD's then-seventeenth president, Rosanne Somerson, responded.

"In order to address the fundamental educational and experiential issues that so many of our students have expressed, particularly our BIPOC students, clear focus needs to be placed on the curriculum and pedagogies," Shenoda detailed. "That shift happens at the faculty level. So, in the case of RISD and the work we are doing through the Center for Social Equity & Inclusion, we are interested not only in bringing on new faculty with particular expertise on issues of race, decoloniality, and non-European practices, but we are trying to build a space through various workshops and initiatives where the relational work of anti-racism can become an active part of faculty, student and staff life," Shenoda further explains.[8]

Edward Fitzpatrick of the *Boston Globe* offers kudos: "Responding to activism, RISD is hiring faculty, boosting diversity....It's one of the most comprehensive attempts by a US college to address racial diversity and equity."[9]

In October 2020, RISD launched its "Race in Art & Design" cluster hire search for ten new faculty as part of an ongoing commitment to address institutional racism and advance social equity. RISD sought faculty members with expertise in the areas of "race, colonization, decolonization, post-coloniality, and cultural representation, as well as in material practices of resistance."

"We repeatedly heard from our community that the most definitive transformation we could make would be to increase the diversity of the scholarship of our faculty and thereby our pedagogy," says Somerson. "This initiative will bring ten new faculty members to RISD in fall 2021, launching a fundamental transformation toward diversifying and expanding our curricula."[10]

RISD more than met the demand for change. After serving RISD for five years as president, Somerson retired in June 2021. In December 2021, Crystal Williams, educator, teacher, and poet, was appointed the eighteenth president of Rhode Island School of Design, becoming the first Black president of any US art and design school. Her tenure began in April 2022.

"Williams' appointment is the culmination of RISD's search for a leader, 'with the global vision to guide RISD's role in helping create a more just, fair and sustainable society.'"[11] Brava!

Decolonizing graphic design history is the primary task in developing a new pedagogy. The needle can't be moved without history and scholarship. We can't decolonize design education without something to decolonize with. From my Black and Brown community's perspective, the challenge with Black design history is the missing pieces; the traditional canon is missing important voices. Many of our stories are sealed away in card catalogs, our memory banks, and our oral traditions. So many histories weren't digitized and didn't make the leap across the technological divide, I contend.

I met Brandon Waybright, who presents the facts. He shows us the problem clearly. Waybright is a designer and educator based near Portland, Oregon, and has served on the board of American Institute of Graphic Arts (AIGA) Portland. He is best known for his podcast, *Full Bleed*, which "explores narrative gaps in design history, education and practice." He analyzes the problem in his data visualization infographic of our design industry's core history book primer. "[Philip B.] Meggs's *History of Graphic Design* remains one of the most-used textbooks on design history, yet it fails to represent the broad range of makers found throughout the world," he says.

"We need to uncover and elevate the stories that are missing from our history....You can't decolonize

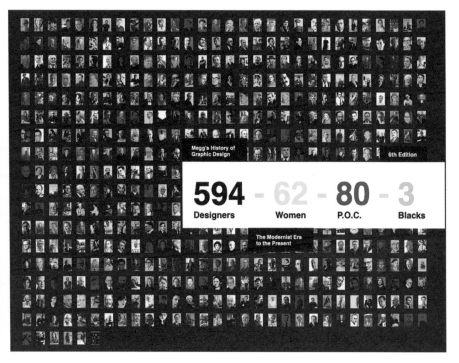

Meggs' History of Graphic Design, 6th ed., designed by Brandon Waybright for Dr. Cheryl D. Miller's 2020 *PRINT* magazine article "Black Designers: Forward in Action, Part IV."

design education without writing a new edition of Meggs's *History of Graphic Design* that includes a global representation beyond 500+ white men." Waybright's popular online infographic displays the Meggs's 6th edition references to 594 designers, of which 62 are women, 80 POC (persons/people of color), and 3 Blacks, leaving 449 white male perspectives to tell the history and formulate pedagogy.

"A few things I noticed along the way: the POC (persons/people of color) count was mostly on account of a section on the Olympics and a section on 'world design' that mostly listed out designers with quick lists. Many women referenced were similarly treated with inclusion in short lists without any information. It felt in many places like the editors were simply trying to get more names in the text," he reflects on problematic representations.

In design, we were raised on white fathers, little to no white mothers, and a few others. It's time to really look at ourselves and this industry, and the expired baby formula and food we were fed. I contend that sophomore-year design studies need to be completely overhauled, with new decolonizing professors and a fresh decolonizing pedagogy. We may never be able to overhaul the entire system, but sophomore year is where you educate and train the new design voices who must not experience the disenfranchising drama of the midcentury historical inadequacies.[12]

Graphic design has predominately been taught from a Eurocentric white male perspective and deeply rooted in the principles of the Bauhaus. But design education is shifting from a Western vantage point to a widely diverse and global perspective. Old histories don't have to reproduce old results; history doesn't have to repeat itself. We can do a new thing, together.

We need a new record of graphic design history. The Academy needs and requires a new sustainable and more inclusive pedagogy—a pedagogy that embraces decolonizing the site map of academia, industry practitioners, and those who will commit to change. Decolonizing, for me, means adding as many lenses as possible to the primary graphic design canon, which

top: **The University of Texas School of Design and Creative Technologies invited me to both develop and teach my course Decolonizing Graphic Design from a Black perspective. I also teach this course at Howard University, as well as the History of Black Graphic Design.** bottom: **Renaissance and Enlightenment graphic design technology—woodcuts, wood and metal type, and letterpress—was used to produce printed material for the transatlantic slave trade.**

has so far had one, primary "white default" focus. Every new design viewpoint, culture, ethnicity, when incorporated, speaks of a brand-new recorded story and history. The new decolonizing scholar is the new design practitioner, the new student, the new historian, the new professor. They will be bringing new twenty-first century pedagogy and practice to our conversation. Breaking the status quo of design thinking for a new and demanding demographic is the charge. It's time to teach a broader story and bring to the table a more diverse as well as inclusive witness to the practice of graphic design.

CHERYL D. HOLMES MILLER is an award-winning designer and holds a master of science–communications design degree from the Pratt Institute, Brooklyn, New York, and a bachelor of fine arts from Maryland Institute College of Art, as well as foundation studies at Rhode Island School of Design. She is the former business owner of Cheryl D. Miller Design, Inc., and has serviced corporate communications to a Fortune 500 clientele. Cheryl's industry honors include induction into The One Club Creative Hall of Fame, 2021 AIGA Medalist for "Expanding Access," 2021 Cooper Hewitt "Design Visionary" National Awardee, 2021 IBM "Eminent Luminary" Honorary Design Scholar, and more. She is also a distinguished design professor at several universities.

—

A portion of this essay appeared in "Black Designers: Forward in Action Part III, and Part IV," *PRINT* magazine.

ACKNOWLEDGMENTS

I embarked on this project because I want to see an industry that does a better job of acknowledging and learning from the beauty and intelligence found within global design practices. I hope that more designers from communities around the globe see themselves represented in this book. I want them to know that they belong in this industry, and that their ideas and approaches to visual communication have value. I also hope that design educators feel excited and supported in their efforts to diversify design pedagogy.

I owe an enormous amount of gratitude to each contributor for their time and commitment to this project. Their work, research, and advocacy is a gift to the design industry. I also want to thank AIGA's Design Educators Community Steering Committee for providing a platform for the *Beyond the Bauhaus* article series to exist. A special thank you to AIGA DEC former cochairs, Meena Khalili and Meaghan Dee, who supported me when I first presented the idea of an article series to them. I'd also like to thank each contributor to the original article series.

A special thank you to Dr. Tiffany Green, who helped me with copyediting throughout the process; to the book's editor, Sara Stemen, who believed this work deserved to be published; and my husband, Jason, for his continuous support.

This book is dedicated to Julian. May you always use your voice for good. Mommy loves you.

NOTES

Chapter 1

1 Kyes Stevens, "Gee's Bend," Encyclopedia of Alabama, updated April 25, 2018, http://www.encyclopediaofalabama.org/article/h-1094.

2 Stevens, "Gee's Bend."

3 Vanessa Kraemer Sohan, "'But a Quilt Is More': Recontextualizing the Discourse(s) of the Gee's Bend Quilts," *College English* 77, no. 4 (March 2015): 294–316.

4 Kraemer Sohan, "'But a Quilt Is More,'" 302.

5 Richard Kalina, "Gee's Bend Modern," *Art in America*, October 2003, 107.

6 Kraemer Sohan, "'But a Quilt Is More,'" 301.

7 Josef Müller-Brockmann, *Grid Systems in Graphic Design: A Visual Communication Manual for Graphic Designers, Typographers, and Three Dimensional Designers*, 4th ed. (Sulgan/Zurich: Verlag Niggli AG, 1981), 11.

8 "Blocks and Stripes Work-Clothes Quilt," Souls Grown Deep Foundation & Community Partnership, accessed August 30, 2022, https://www.soulsgrowndeep.org/artist/missouri-pettway/work/blocks-and-strips-work-clothes-quilt.

9 *Quiltmakers of Gee's Bend*, Alabama Public Television Documentaries, aired May 1, 2004, https://www.pbs.org/video/alabama-public-television-documentaries-quiltmakers-of-gees-bend/.

10 bell hooks, *Belonging: A Culture of Place* (New York: Routledge, 1990), 163.

Chapter 4

1 Dugald Stermer, and Susan Sontag, *The Art of Revolution: 96 Posters from Cuba* (London: Pall Mall Press, 1970).

2 "The Harsh Sentencing of Human Rights Defenders in Cuba," press release, US Department of State, June 30, 2022, https://www.state.gov/the-harsh-sentencing-of-human-rights-defenders-in-cuba/.

3 "List of Countries by Incarceration Rate," Wikipedia, accessed July 14, 2022, https://en.wikipedia.org/w/index.php?title=List_of_countries_by_incarceration_rate&oldid=1092114831.

4 Ada Ferrer, *Cuba: An American History* (New York: Scribner, 2021), 391.

5 Fernando Camacho Padilla y Eugenia Palieraki, "¡Hasta siempre, OSPAAAL!," NACLA, January 16, 2020, https://nacla.org/news/2020/01/16/hasta-siempre-ospaaal-havana-cuba.

6 *NOW!*, directed by Santiago Álvarez (ICAIC, 1965), https://vimeo.com/425196856?embedded=true&source=video_title&owner=38668286.

7 Shanti Escalante-De Mattei, "Tania Bruguera Agrees to Leave Cuba in Exchange for Release of Prisoners," *ARTnews*, October 11, 2021, https://www.artnews.com/art-news/news/tania-bruguera-cuba-release-prisoners-1234606644/.

8 "El Paquete Semanal (The Weekly Package), or El Paquete, is a one-terabyte collection of digital material distributed since around 2008 on the underground market in Cuba as a substitute for broadband Internet. Since 2015, it has been the primary source of entertainment for millions of Cubans, as Internet in Cuba has been suppressed for many years, with only about a 38.8 percent Internet penetration rate as of 2018." https://en.wikipedia.org/wiki/El_Paquete_Semanal, Accessed July 22, 2022.

Chapter 5

1 Anne-Marie Deisser and Lolan Sipan, "Decorative Art or Art Practice? The Conservation of Textiles in the Kurdish Autonomous Region of Iraq," *Studies in Conservation* 57, no. sup1 (2012): S80–S86, https://doi.org/10.1179/20470584 12y.0000000025.

2 Deisser and Sipan, "Decorative Art."

3 A gul is the flower of a rose. In conversation, we refer to all flowers as *gul*, but the proper word for flower in Kurdish is *kulik*. -*Stan* means "land" or "the place of" (but in English slang can mean someone who is a devoted fan). *Gulistan* means "land of the flowers," though when translated verbatim to English, it is "flower land." It can also be poetically rephrased as "flowers of the land." It is also a common name for women in Kurdistan. Gulê is the appellation used for Gulistan.

4 Examples of this were exquisitely discussed in the first chapter of bell hooks's *Feminist Theory: From Margin to Center*. hooks states that white feminists often assume Black women were unaware of sexist oppression until white women expressed their feminist ideas. They think they are delivering *the* insight and *the* blueprint for liberation. They

don't realize, or can't imagine, that Black women, like other groups of women who live in oppressive situations daily, often develop an awareness of patriarchal politics because of their lived experience, just as they develop resistance strategies, even if they don't resist on a sustained or organized basis.

5 David Ebony and ARTbooks, *Patterns of Promiscuity: The Pattern and Decoration Movement in American Art of the 1970s and '80s* (New Haven, CT: Yale University Press, 2020) https://yalebooks.yale.edu/2020/05/26/patterns-of-promiscuity-the-pattern-and-decoration-movement-in-american-art-of-the-1970s-and-80s/.

6 Ebony and ARTbooks, "Patterns of Promiscuity."

7 In the book *Artist as Culture Producer*, by Sharon Louden, the artist Jean Shin described her relationship to collecting materials from a larger community in the following quote that deeply resonated with me: "Inviting participation from a community through a request for materials did a few key things for my work: it activated a social interaction with people unknown to me (and often unfamiliar with art), while creating an audience invested in the exhibition. It also meant that the museum or other commissioning venue would facilitate material acquisition and become an active part of my art making. This collaboration allows individuals to share personal stories behind the objects that they donate, generating a richer narrative around the work." Sharon Louden, *Artist as Culture Producer: Living and Sustaining a Creative Life* (Chicago: Intellect, 2017), 192.

Chapter 6

1 Nadja Sayej, "AfriCOBRA: The Collective That Helped Shape the Black Arts Movement," *Guardian*, June 14, 2018, https://www.theguardian.com/artanddesign/2018/jun/15/africobra-now-exhibition-new-york-black-arts-movement.

2 Antwaun Sargent, "Arthur Jafa and the Future of Black Cinema," Interview, January 11, 2017, https://www.interviewmagazine.com/art/arthur-jafa.

3 "Gullah Geechee Cultural Heritage Corridor," National Park Service, US Department of the Interior, https://www.nps.gov/places/gullah-geechee-cultural-heritage-corridor.htm. Accessed August 18, 2022.

4 Erik Sherman, "Median Wealth of Black and Latino Families Could Hit Zero by the Middle of the Century," *Forbes*, September 11, 2017, https://www.forbes.com/sites/eriksherman/2017/09/11/median-wealth-of-black-and-latino-families-could-hit-zero-before-the-centurys-end.

5 "HUD Releases 2021 Annual Homeless Assessment Report Part 1," press release, US Department of Housing and Urban Development, February 4, 2022, https://www.hud.gov/press/press_releases_media_advisories/hud_no_22_022.

6 "Quick Facts: United States," United States Census Bureau, accessed August 18, 2022, https://www.census.gov/quickfacts/fact/table/US/PST045221.

7 "The Color of Wealth in Boston," The Samuel DuBois Cook Center on Social Equity, accessed August 18, 2022, https://socialequity.duke.edu/portfolio-item/the-color-of-wealth-in-boston/.

8 Neil Bhutta, Andrew C. Chang, Lisa J. Dettling, and Joanne W. Hsu with assistance from Julia Hewitt, "Disparities in Wealth by Race and Ethnicity in the 2019 Survey of Consumer Finances," September 28, 2020, https://www.federalreserve.gov/econres/notes/feds-notes/disparities-in-wealth-by-race-and-ethnicity-in-the-2019-survey-of-consumer-finances-20200928.htm.

9 Marie Gørrild, Sharon Obialo, and Nienke Venema, "Gentrification and Displacement in Harlem: How the Harlem Community Lost Its Voice En Route to Progress," Knowledge Resources, Humanity in Action, https://humanityinaction.org/knowledge_detail/gentrification-and-displacement-in-harlem-how-the-harlem-community-lost-its-voice-en-route-to-progress/.

Chapter 7

1 Ami Kantawala, "Art Education in Colonial India: Implementation and Imposition," *Studies in Art Education* 53, no. 3 (2021): 209.

2 Kantawala, "Art Education," 212.

3 Kantawala, "Art Education," 216.

4 Habiba Insaf, "Indian Calendar Art: The Popular Picture Story," openDemocracy, last modified April 10, 2012, https://www.opendemocracy.net/en/openindia/indian-calendar-art-popular-picture-story/.

5 Seema Srivastava, pers. comm., May 30, 2012.

6 Balkaar Singh, pers. comm., May 12, 2012.

7 Raja Gharu, pers. comm., June 8, 2012.

8 Mohammad Anwar, pers. comm., June 6, 2012.

9 Seema Srivastava, pers. comm., May 30, 2012.

10 Prasanna Sankhé, pers. comm., June 22, 2012.

11 Juhoor Ahmed, pers. comm., June 2, 2012.

12 Mohammed Ashraf, pers. comm., June 7, 2012.

13 Merriam-Webster, s.v. "vernacular," accessed July 17, 2022, https://www.merriam-webster.com/dictionary/vernacular.

14 World of Dictionary, s.v. "verna," accessed July 17, 2022, https://worldofdictionary.com/dict/latin-english/meaning/verna.

15 Vaibhav Singh, "The Machine in the Colony: Technology, Politics, and the Typography of Devanagari in the Early Years of Mechanization," *Philological Encounters* 3, no. 4 (2018): 472.

16 Kantawala, "Art Education," 211.

17 Rahul Mhaiskar, "Romanagari an Alternative for Modern Media Writings," *Bulletin of the Deccan College Research Institute* 75 (2015): 196.

Chapter 8

1 Beatriz Colomina and Mark Wigley, *Are We Human? Notes on an Archaeology of Design* (Zurich, Switzerland: Lars Müller Publishers, 2017), 9.

2 Fatima Sadiqi, *Moroccan Feminist Discourses* (New York: Palgrave Macmillan, 2014), 61.

3 Bruno Barbatti, *Berber Carpets of Morocco: The Symbols, Origin, and Meaning* (Courbevoie, France: ACR Edition Internationale, 2008), 16.

4 Barbatti, *Berber Carpets*, 10–16; Sadiqi, *Moroccan Feminist Discourses*, 41.

5 Sadiqi, *Moroccan Feminist Discourses*, 46.

6 "Spanish Morocco," Encyclopedia.Com, accessed February 17, 2022, https://www.encyclopedia.com/history/asia-and-africa/north-african-history/spanish-morocco.

7 Magdi Abdelhadi, "Ceuta and Melilla: Spain's Enclaves in North Africa," Africa, *BBC News*, June 5, 2021, https://www.bbc.com/news/world-africa-57305882.

8 Lisa Bernasek, "The Taste for Moroccan Arts in Paris, 1917–2006" (paper presented at Middle East Studies Association Annual Conference, Boston, November 18, 2006), https://eprints.soton.ac.uk/181405/.

9 Silvia Gagliardi, *Minority Rights, Feminism, and International Law: Voices of Amazigh Women in Morocco* (New York: Routledge, 2020), 136.

10 Hamza Cherif D'Ouezzan, online interview by author, February 15, 2022. In my discussion with Hamza, he wanted me to mention in my writing that his title does not reflect the fact that the weavers are the true leaders of the Anou, since they work with a horizontal dynamic rather than a top-down approach.

11 Myriem Naji, "Learning to Weave the Threads of Honor: Understanding the Value of Female Schooling in Southern Morocco," *Anthropology & Education Quarterly* 43, no. 4 (December 2012): 372, https://doi.org/10.1111/.

12 Naji, "Learning to Weave," 373–82.

13 Cherif D'Ouezzan, online interview.

14 Myriem Naji, "Gender and Materiality in-the-Making: The Manufacture of

Sirwan Femininities through Weaving in Southern Morocco," *Journal of Material Culture* 14, no. 1 (March 2009): 69, https://doi.org/10.1177/1359183508100008.

15 Naji, "Gender and Materiality," 69.

16 Yassine Marouani, "Indicateurs de l'artisanat—Ministère du Tourisme, de l'artisanat et de l'economie sociale et solidaire," Royaume du Maroc, accessed March 26, 2022, https://mtaess-gov-ma.translate.goog/fr/artisanat/observatoire/?_x_tr_sl=fr&_x_tr_tl=en&_x_tr_hl=en&_x_tr_pto=sc/.

17 Marouani, "Indicateurs de l'artisanat."

18 Oulaghada, online interview, January 9, 2022.

19 Oulaghada, interview.

20 "About Us and FAQ," Anou, accessed March 26, 2022, http://www.theanou.com/about.

21 Brinkley Messick, "Subordinate Discourse: Women, Weaving, and Gender Relations in North Africa," *American Ethnologist* 14, no. 2 (May 1987): 220, https://doi.org/10.1525/ae.1987.14.2.02a00020.

22 Cherif D'Ouezzan, online interview.

23 Cherif D'Ouezzan, online interview.

24 Cherif D'Ouezzan, online interview; and Anou, "Refining the Vision of Anou," *The Anou Cooperative Blog*, June 22, 2016, https://helloanou.wordpress.com/2016/06/22/refining-the-vision-of-anou/.

25 Sadiqi, *Moroccan Feminist Discourses*, 154.

26 Cynthia Becker, "Amazigh Textiles and Dress in Morocco Metaphors of Motherhood," *African Arts* 39, no. 3 (October 1, 2006): 52, https://doi.org/10.1162/afar.2006.39.3.42.

27 "The Story of Carpets in Morocco: The Magic behind Berber Rugs," Zarabe, accessed March 8, 2022, https://zarabe.com/blogs/news/the-moroccan-berber-rug-an-abstract-art.

28 Anou, "What Is the Difference between a Flatweave, Pile Knot, and Beni Ourain Rug?," *The Anou Cooperative Blog*, August 23, 2014, https://helloanou.wordpress.com/2014/08/23/what-is-the-difference-between-flatweave-pile-knot-and-beni-ourain-rugs/.

29 "Story of Carpets in Morocco."

30 "Story of Carpets in Morocco."

31 "Story of Carpets in Morocco."

32 Becker, "Amazigh Textiles," 48.

Chapter 13

1 Jeffrey S. Passel, Gretchen Livingston, and D'Vera Cohn, "Explaining Why Minority Births Now Outnumber White Births," Pew Research Center, May 17, 2012, www.pewresearch.org/social-trends/2012/05/17/explaining-why-minority-births-now-outnumber-white-births/; Bill Chappell, "For U.S. Children, Minorities Will Be the Majority by 2020, Census Says," *The Two-Way*, NPR, March 4, 2015, www.npr.org/sections/thetwo-way/2015/03/04/390672196/for-u-s-children-minorities-will-be-the-majority-by-2020-census-says; Dudley Poston and Rogelio Sáenz, "The US White Majority Will Soon Disappear Forever," *Chicago Reporter*, May 16, 2019, www.chicagoreporter.com/

the-us-white-majority-will-soon-disappear-forever/.

2 Jason Duaine Hahn, "2020 Census Data Shows White Population in the U.S. Declined for First Time on Record," *People*, August 12, 2021, https://people.com/human-interest/census-shows-white-population-in-us-has-declined/.

3 Kymberly Pinder, in discussion with author, 2022.

4 "ACAID Statement of Principles on Diversity, Equity, and Inclusion," AICAD, accessed October 17, 2022, www.aicad.org/principles-on-dei/.

5 Deborah Obalil and Elissa Tenny, "AICAD Stands with HBCUs against Violence and Intimidation," AICAD, accessed October 17, 2022, www.aicad.org/wp-content/uploads/2022-02-03_AICAD-HBCU_SupportLtr.pdf.

6 Erin N. S. Unkefer, Connor Curtis, Lucia Andrade, Cayla Tepper, and Nikole Barnes, "'Out of My Element': The Experiences of Black Art Students in Critique," *Journal of Diversity in Higher Education* (2021), https://doi.org/10.1037/dhe0000322.

7 Jada Akatao, "RISD and Race Forum" (forum at Rhode Island School of Design, June 16, 2020), digitalcommons.risd.edu/archives_activism_racialjustice/20/.

8 Cheryl D. Holmes-Miller, "Black Designers: Forward in Action (Part III)," *Print*, October 8, 2020, https://www.printmag.com/design-education/black-designers-forward-in-action-part-iii/.

9 Edward Fitzpatrick, "Responding to Activism, RISD Is Hiring Faculty, Boosting Diversity, Returning Looted Artifacts," *Boston Globe*, July 21, 2020, www.bostonglobe.com/2020/07/21/metro/responding-activism-risd-is-hiring-faculty-boosting-diversity-returning-looted-sculpture/.

10 "RISD Launches 'Race in Art & Design' Cluster Hire Search," Rhode Island School of Design, October 5, 2020, https://www.risd.edu/news/stories/risd-launches-cluster-hire-search.

11 Cajsa Carlson, "Crystal Williams Named First Black President of Rhode Island School of Design," Dezeen, December 16, 2021, https://www.dezeen.com/2021/12/16/crystal-williams-black-president-rhode-island-school-of-design/.

12 Cheryl D. Holmes-Miller, "Black Designers: Forward in Action (Part IV)," *Print*, October 15, 2020, https://www.printmag.com/design-news/black-designers-forward-in-action-part-iv/.

CREDITS